Place names
in Ulster

**JONATHAN
BARDON**

ULSTER HISTORICAL
FOUNDATION

Acknowledgements

Ulster Historical Foundation would like to thank all the patrons, donors and subscribers to this volume who are listed at the end of this book. Without their generous financial support publication would not have been possible. We are most grateful for their contributions.

The Foundation would also like to thank Carol Tweedale Bardon and the Northern Ireland Council for the Curriculum, Examinations and Assessment (CCEA) on behalf of the former Northern Ireland Centre for Learning Resources (NICLR) for permission to republish this work. In particular we wish to thank Brian McAleese (CCEA) who helped to secure permission for this new edition.
In addition, we are grateful to Carol for contributing her personal, thoughtful Foreword.
We are indebted to Dr Kay Muhr for her informative introduction and advice on an extended reading list, which she readily agreed to deliver despite competing deadlines, and also to Angélique Day, Gillian Hunt, Dr Éamon Phoenix and Dr William Roulston for their advice, assistance and input. Special thanks also goes to the staff at the Public Record Office Northern Ireland, especially Grace Gordon, and also to Ian Montgomery (formerly of PRONI) for assistance with images of sources. The Northern Ireland Place-Name Project and Ulster Place-Name Society gave permission to draw material from their published and online resources for this publication. Wendy Dunbar has again excelled in producing a contemporary and eye-catching layout, building on what was already a visually-appealing original design by NICLR. Finally, we would like to acknowledge Gerry Mullan who made the suggestion that the Foundation might republish this work as a small tribute to a greatly admired and respected historian and author.

The Foundation would like to apologise in advance for any errors or omissions. If material has been used without proper acknowledgment we will seek to rectify such oversights in any future reprint.

Letter to Lady Londonderry from Sir Herbert Maxwell (PRONI, D3099/3/19/1/7), p. 31; and 'Scotch Quarter' from 'A Survey of the Town of Downpatrick in the County of Down … by James Maguire, 1708' (PRONI, D477/1), p. 51, reproduced courtesy of the Deputy Keeper of the Records, Public Record Office of Northern Ireland.

FRONT COVER PHOTOGRAPH
Road sign Glangevlin, near the Shannon source, Co. Cavan, March 1991
(Courtesy Sludge G, Flickr, www.flickr.com/photos/sludgeulper/4037376243)

INSIDE COVER ILLUSTRATION
'A Generalle Description of Ulster', 1603, by Richard Bartlett
(MPF 1/35 TNA)

First published as *Investigating Place Names in Ulster: A Teachers' Guide* in 1991,
by Northern Ireland Centre for Learning Resources (NICLR)
republished as *Place Names in the North of Ireland* in 1992
by NICLR, distributed by NI-CO Education Services

This edition published as *Place names in Ulster*
by Ulster Historical Foundation in 2020.

www.ancestryireland.com
www.booksireland.org.uk

ISBN (2020 edition): 978-1-909556-87-4

PRINTED BY
GPS Colour Graphics Ltd

REVISED DESIGN
Dunbar Design

Contents

Foreword

Jonathan Bardon

Maybe you are just visiting Ulster, maybe you have lived here for many years or maybe you, and generations before you, were born here, but know little about who established the settlement you are now visiting, living in or were born in. As you will find from this book the name of the settlement is often the clue to its history.

Although born in Dublin and living there until he finished Trinity College, Jonathan's family had many ties with Ulster but it was probably still a surprise when he made his way to Belfast in 1963 and settled there. While teaching boys, who called him the Irish teacher, in Belfast in the 1960s, talking to colleagues and new friends in Belfast he came to realise that the boys, their families, the wider community and he himself needed to learn and understand much more about the history of Ulster. 'I noticed that many of the pupils were sons of men who worked in some of the great industries in east Belfast, like the shipyard and the ropeworks, but they knew very little about what was once a world-renowned industrial powerhouse.'

So he began his life-long research into Ulster history and his determination to share his knowledge and understanding by writing as well as teaching. Jonathan's writings are accessible and his knowledge wide: from pre-historic times, when people first came to Ireland, to today; from the migrations of plants and animals, to the migrations of peoples. The names of places, as we will read in this book, give insight into these migrations, where the people came from and where they settled.

Jonathan always wished for his writing to contribute to improved community harmony in Ulster. Reputed for a balanced approach in his many books, it was always an aim of Jonathan to show to the reader that the people of this divided province have a shared past and the community divisions are not based on nature or genes – we are not simply a Planter or a Gael. He frequently pointed out that family names in Ulster indicate considerable intermarriage between the communities in the past, and that place names show the widespread distribution of migrants to Ulster over many centuries. This book, explaining the Irish Celtic (Gaelic), Viking, Anglo-Norman and Plantation roots of many of our familiar Ulster place names, most certainly illustrates his latter point.

If you enjoy exploring the Ulster countryside, as Jonathan and I often did, this book will be an easily accessible guide to the backgrounds of the people who established the townland, village, town or city you are passing through. There are photographs to stimulate your curiosity and maps to guide your journey. Maybe this book will provide you with all you want to know or maybe it will be a stimulant and guide for further and future in-depth research.

I had Jonathan beside me bringing the history of places and their names to life – you have this book.

CAROL TWEEDALE BARDON

Introduction

I am delighted to be asked to introduce a new generation of students to this reprint of Jonathan Bardon's *Investigating Place Names in Ulster* (1991). Jonathan was a great friend of place-name studies and I was very pleased when he invited me to comment on his text before it went to press. Almost all my suggestions he took on board, with gracious acknowledgement, and strong promotion (in his Further Investigation section) of the aims of the Northern Ireland Place-Name Project at Queen's University, where I worked from its foundation in 1987 to 2010. To reprint *Investigating Place Names in Ulster* now is timely, not least because it coincides with renewed activity by the Northern Ireland Place-Name Project, which since 1992 has produced books, and a website (2004) giving information on the names (www.placenamesni.org), as well as Facebook and Twitter accounts.

Jonathan well understood the importance of 'naming'. Names are our basic building blocks in all research, and history takes place in a landscape of named people and places. His guide, published well before the Belfast/Good Friday Agreement, deals carefully with the sensitivities of the time: what is Ulster?; who named its places?; are the names 'Theirs' or 'Ours'? He tells the history of the Celtic Gaels and the nine-county Ulster, the Vikings (few place-names), the Anglo-Normans, the Gaelic Scots and the English and Scots settlers of the Plantation, with a full introduction to Irish-Gaelic place-name terminology. Perhaps he might have emphasised more how medieval Irish society was accustomed to several languages: there was the Latin of the Church; the formerly French-speaking Normans were only recently English-speaking, who learned Irish too when useful; and some Scottish Plantation settlers used Scottish Gaelic as well as dialects of Scots. Despite historians' shorthand of peoples 'overwhelming' others, Jonathan points out that many Celtic place-names survive in Europe, that often the Normans 'simply used the native Irish place-names', re-spelled; and that Plantation settlers 'usually retained' the anglicised Gaelic (townland) names in the grants that gave them title to land. The guide ends with the names of 'new' Plantation towns, taverns and streets, and small local features, likely to be created in English.

A suggestion not followed by Jonathan, but still relevant today, was the need to explain the significance of townlands – the small administrative area unique to Ireland. In the 1970s the Post Office of the United Kingdom, accustomed to English-type settlement in villages, adopted a policy of omitting townland names from Northern Ireland addresses. In 1990, the Federation of Ulster Local Studies (including the Ulster Place-Name Society[1]) was waging the 'Save our Townlands' campaign, with stalwarts like Cathal Dallat, Harry Hume and Jack Johnston taking the platform, which I was sometimes invited to share. In Jonathan's guide, fuller description of the thousand-year history of the townland system would have better supported the campaign, and also avoided the common confusion about the word 'town' in 'townland', and 'Bally' in place-names (p. 16). Irish *baile* still does not so much mean a modern 'town' as a 'place', and earlier meant 'homestead, farm, settlement'. Interestingly, this is very similar to the history of English town (*tūn*) which also meant 'farmstead' (compare Scots *ferm-toun*) before it came to mean a larger settlement. The townland was the commonly-used small unit to describe land-holding at the Plantation and across Ulster over 16,000 named townlands survive, as explained subsequently in *Celebrating Ulster's Townlands*.[2]

It is worth recalling in a little more detail just how difficult the times were for a pioneering venture such as Jonathan's. The Ulster Place-Name Society (founded in 1952) had long put forward that the history of place-names in Northern Ireland deserved serious research, as was already happening for place-names in the Republic. The Northern Ireland Place-Name Project in Queen's University Belfast was founded following the Anglo-Irish Agreement of 1985, and it was rumoured that the study of (all the) place-names was the closest that government could get to showing any interest in the Irish language. About the same time the Northern Ireland Education Minister Brian Mawhinney was consulting on what became the 1989 Education Reform (NI) Order, which would require all schools for the first time to follow a common curriculum, including two cross-curricular themes in which place-name study would prove central: Education for Mutual Understanding (EMU) and Cultural Heritage (CH). Having served with characteristic skill and good humour as the Chairman of the Working Groups that developed these themes, Jonathan was seconded by the Department of Education to write *Investigating Place Names in Ulster*, as a resource for teachers, and it was duly published by the Northern Ireland Centre for Learning Resources, based at Stranmillis College.

I got to know Jonathan further at the end of the 1990s, when his colleague Aidan McGoarty invited me to Belcoo in Fermanagh to talk on local townland names, followed by poetry and music. This occasion set the pattern for several place-name tours during the annual Cathal Buí Mac Giolla Gunna Festival, to which Jonathan was regularly invited to give an evening lecture on Irish history. The festival was a happy time of company and talk in beautiful and hospitable surroundings, and the subject often turned to place-names, including the names of fishing pools, since Jonathan was a keen fisherman who knew his waterways well.

A memorable fishing place to him was Lough Melvin nearby, between Leitrim and Fermanagh, containing four distinct strains of fresh-water trout: brown, gillaroo, sonaghan and ferox, which each play their own separate part in a balanced ecosystem. In an article for the Northern Ireland Community Relations Council[3], Jonathan suggested that the diversity of the trout might be a metaphor for the diversity of the different historical communities now co-existing in Ireland (although members of these, unlike the fish, have managed to marry across the divide). The names of the four types of trout might also be taken as a metaphor for our languages and their place-names: English (brown); Latin (*ferox* 'fierce'), and Irish (gillaroo being *giolla rua* 'russet lad', and sonaghan, *samhnachán*). Interestingly, the meaning of this last (used in Mayo for sea-trout), is obscure, and there is no simple connection with the also-unexplained *sewen*, the word for sea-trout in Welsh, Cornish and Breton. The Irish seems most likely to mean 'Novemberling', referring to the return of sea-trout in autumn to their spawning grounds, but if this is so the Lough Melvin usage has shifted in meaning.[4]

Normally, the languages of place-names do not mix, except when one name is used to explain or identify another, as in names like Sruhananess Burn, from Irish *Sruthán* an *Easa* 'stream of the waterfall'. However, the languages of Irish, English and Scots are woven together in the damask fabric of the place-name landscape of Ulster. To that landscape Jonathan provided an enticing and well-illustrated guide. May its reprinting entice a new generation of researchers to join the continuing investigation.

KAY MUHR

1 Ulster Place-Name Society, www.ulsterplacename.org.
2 Kay Muhr, *Celebrating Ulster's Townlands* (Belfast: Ulster Place-Name Society, 1999). An illustrated A4 booklet (32 pp) to accompany the Ulster Place-Name Society travelling exhibition for the Millennium.
3 Jonathan Bardon, 'From the earliest times to the Union' in Maurna Crozier and Richard Froggatt (eds), *What made now in Northern Ireland* (Belfast: Northern Ireland Community Relations Council, 2008).
4 With thanks to Ciarán Ó Duibhín for his help with the Irish language references to fish.

Place names
in **Ulster**

JONATHAN BARDON

Introduction

The investigation of local place names can be an enjoyable and rewarding experience. Though scholars have to have a very thorough knowledge of all the languages once spoken in an area before they can interpret its place names, those who are not experts should not be discouraged.

Most of the older place names in Ulster were originally in Irish Celtic (Gaelic), but if you have no Irish this book will provide you with some of the key terms used in place names, and a bibliography for further reading.

The nineteenth-century Ordnance Survey, working from the evidence of old spellings and local pronunciation, tried to give the same Irish word the same spelling each time, in the English forms, on their maps, It was not always possible, however, to discover what the Irish word had been. Today the pronunciation used by local people can be very helpful in the investigation of place names - it may represent the original form more closely than does the spelling. Ask an English visitor to pronounce Ahoghill or Portglenone and this will usually produce peals of laughter from local people who may not know a word of Irish. And yet local pronunciation is very close to the original Irish. That is not to say that problems cannot arise. Is Broughshane pronounced **brock-shane** or **bruh-shane**? Even people who live there cannot agree.

A final point: as this book attempts to show, many Ulster place names are not Gaelic at all (around 50% in Co Down, for example).

How Ulster got its name

At the beginning of the Christian era Cúige Uladh, 'the Fifth of the Ulstermen', was the northern province of Ireland, divided from the 'Fifths' or provinces of Connacht and Meath by a line running from the mouth of the Drowes river (near Bundoran in Co Donegal) to the estuary of the river Boyne at Drogheda. Its rulers were called the **Ulaidh** (pronounced 'ully', to rhyme with 'bully'), a tribal name recorded by Ptolemy about 150 AD as **Voluntii**.

The people of Ulster were descended from those who had settled the north from about 7,000 BC: Mesolithic, Neolithic and Bronze Age peoples and a variety of Iron Age invaders who were speaking Irish or Gaelic when Christianity was brought to Ulster in the fifth century AD. In the great Gaelic epic tale, the "Cattle Raid of Cooley", the men of Ulster defeated Queen Maeve and her Connachtmen. We know, however, that the Ulaidh suffered a series of defeats and from about the fifth century AD to about the eighth century AD the rulers of the Ulaidh held sway over no more than the present counties of Antrim and Down.

The Vikings called the land of the Ulaidh, 'Uladztír'- they mixed their own pronunciation with the Irish word **tír**, which means 'land'. When the Normans and the English began to invade the north towards the end of the twelfth century they adopted the Viking version just as they did with **Lein-ster, Mun-ster and Ire-land**. And so in time **Uladztír** became anglicised to **Ulster**.

Throughout the later Middle Ages the Irish and the English alike regarded Ulster as a province which was the whole of the north, including the Carlingford peninsula in Co Louth. The frontier was finally set by the Lord Deputy Sir Henry Sidney in the reign of Queen Elizabeth I and the shapes of the nine counties of the province of Ulster were decided in 1611. Those counties are Antrim, Down, Tyrone, Londonderry, Armagh, Fermanagh, Donegal, Cavan and Monaghan. In 1920 Northern Ireland was created out of the first six of the nine counties listed. Thus while Northern Ireland is often spoken of as "Ulster" or "the province", strictly speaking it is only part of the historic province of Ulster.

Mouth of the river Drowes

LONDONDERRY

ANTRIM

DONEGAL

TYRONE

DOWN

FERMANAGH

ARMAGH

MONAGHAN

Carlingford Peninsula

CAVAN

LOUTH

Mouth of the river Boyne

Province of Ulster	
Northern Ireland	——————
County borders	——————

Who named places in Ulster?

The overwhelming majority of Ulster's place names are Gaelic in origin. The Vikings left their mark only on a handful of places in the north. Only very few of the names Norman invaders gave to places in Ulster have survived. Hebridean Scots may have been responsible for naming many places in Ulster - especially in the Glens of Antrim - but it is almost impossible to distinguish their place names from those of the native Irish since they all spoke the one language of Gaelic. Scots Gaelic and Irish Gaelic used the same written form until the late seventeenth century.

The English and Lowland Scots who settled Ulster in great numbers from the beginning of the seventeenth century onwards all spoke English, though in a wide variety of dialects and accents. These colonists were often content to keep Gaelic place names, though under anglicised spellings, since these appeared in the official grants which gave them legal title to the land; **Beal Feirsde** (meaning the mouth of, or approach to the sandbank) became Belfast. However, many of the leading English and Scots planters did give new names to a wide variety of towns, estates and other places in Ulster, such as Hilltown, Draperstown and Richill. Since then developers and local councils have had to coin new names for housing estates, streets, bridges, etc - for example there are streets in Belfast named after Prime Ministers, World War generals and ships; Harmony Heights near Lisburn; and Craigavon, named after Northern Ireland's first Prime Minister.

Irish or Gaelic place names in Ulster

What is Irish? In simple terms it was the language spoken by most people in Ireland until the early nineteenth century. The language is called **Gaeilge,** anglicised as Gaelic, which survives most successfully as a spoken language in parts of Donegal, Connemara and Kerry.

Gaelic is a Celtic language - but who were the Celts? The Celts were the first people north of the Alps to emerge into recorded history. Their distinctive culture evolved during the second millenium BC between Bohemia and the east bank of the Rhine and then spread north towards Denmark, south-east into the Balkans, south to Italy, and west to France, northern Spain, Portugal, the Low Countries, Britain and Ireland. They also reached Asia Minor - St Paul's Epistle to the Galatians was written to Celts settled in Anatolia. Later still Celts, in this case Irish monks, were the first human beings to reach the Faeroes and Iceland. It is more difficult to trace the language since writing was little used by the Celts in pagan times.

Eventually Roman conquest and German migration overwhelmed the Celts on the European mainland but many of their place names survive, such as Rhine, Danube, Vienna, Seine and Paris. **Lugh** the sun god had been revered by the Celts and his name is incorporated in place names across Europe, such as **Leon** (Spain), **London** (England), **Leiden** (Netherlands), **Lyons** (France), **Legnica** (Poland), **and Louth** (Ireland).

Evidence shows that the Celtic language spoken in Roman times was very like Latin. There were also two main varieties, Q-Celtic and P-Celtic. Q-Celtic became the form used in Ireland, which survives as Gaelic, P-Celtic in Britain surviving as Welsh, and in France as Breton.

Gaelic continued to evolve; for example the personal name **Cunagusos** in the fourth century AD had become **Congus** by the seventh century AD and, over the same period, the word **velitas** - meaning a poet - had become **file**. Thereafter the **filí**, the professional class of poets, did much to ensure the remarkable uniformity of the Irish language. It was probably not until the fifteenth century that English had reached the same level of standardisation. Irish expansion, spearheaded by the north Antrim kingdom of Dál Riata in the fifth century, extended the use of Gaelic to the Isle of Man and across the Islands and Highlands of Scotland. To the medieval Irish the North Channel, 'the straits of Moyle', was a passage and not a frontier; to them the Gael of Ireland and of Scotland were but one people.

The difference between 'Q-Celtic' and 'P-Celtic' can be shown by looking at the word for headland: **ceann** anglicised as **ken** or **kin** in Q-Celtic, with a Q or K sound, and incorporated in such place names as Kenmare, Kinsale, Kenbane Head, Kintyre and Kinlochleven; and **pen** as a prefix in such Welsh and Cornish place names as Penryn, Penarth, Penrith and Penzance. The 'ken' words are Gaelic and the 'pen' words are 'Brittonic' - the P-Celtic once spoken by the Ancient Britons and now surviving in modern form in Wales and Brittany.

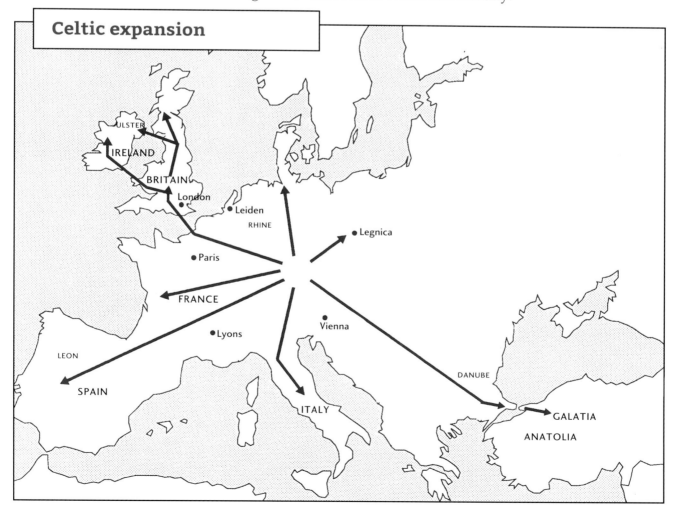

Celtic expansion

NORTHERN IRELAND TOURIST BOARD

The Mountains of Mourne

Kingdoms and peoples

Early Irish society consisted of many small tribal kingdoms, some grouped under an over-king, or the king of a province such as Ulster. The names of these early population groups may appear in the names of places, in the land they once owned. Some of these tribal kingdoms were the size of the old subdivision of a county called a barony, and population names are common in barony and county names.

The oldest type are plurals such as **Ulaidh**, 'Ulstermen', and **Cruthin**, 'Britons' (**Cruthin** is the Q-Celtic form of **Pritani** or **Prydyn**, from whom Britain is named, and this tribe, important in eastern Ulster, may have migrated from Britain). Another type added the suffix **-raige**, meaning 'the people of'; for example the **Dartraige** (who gave their name to the barony of Dartry in Co Monaghan) were the 'calf people'. Others are obscure in meaning including names ending in **-ne**, such as the **Eilne** who lived between the Bush and the Bann rivers, and the **Latharne**, who gave their name to Larne.

* Later peoples, perhaps pushed west to Ireland by the might of Rome, called themselves after their supernatural ancestors and their tribal names have the suffix **-achta**, meaning 'the followers of': for example the **Ciannachta** (who gave their name to Keenaght, the northern barony of Co Londonderry) were 'the followers of Cian'. The **Connachta**, who gave their name to Ireland's western province, were 'the followers of Conn', a wolf god long worshipped on the European mainland. Their ruling family, the **Uí Néill**, traced their descent from Niall of the Nine Hostages who is usually credited with the conquest of most of Ulster west of the river Bann around the fifth century AD.

Another name applied to kingdoms was **tír**, meaning 'land'. For example, **Tír Eoghain**, after which the present county of Tyrone is named, was 'the land of Eoghan', one of the sons of Niall of the Nine Hostages.

Some peoples - usually ruling families - called themselves **fir**, 'the men'. For example, **Fir Manach**, after whom the present county of Fermanagh is named, were 'the men of Manach', found in Ptolemy's map as **Menapii**.

The smallest type of kingdom in Gaelic Ireland was the **tuath** (a word related to the English 'teutonic' and the German 'Deutsch'), a territory generally the size of a barony such as Oneilland in Co Armagh or Kinelarty in Co Down.

* English example: the place name Hastings derives from the Anglo-Saxon **Hastingas**, 'the followers as Hasta'.

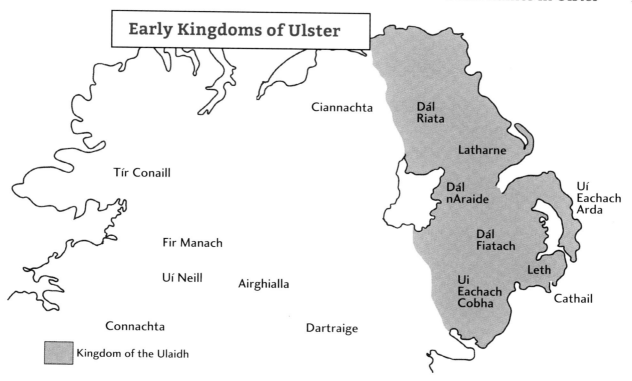

Early Kingdoms of Ulster

Ciannachta

Dál Riata

Latharne

Tír Conaill

Dál nAraide

Uí Eachach Arda

Fir Manach

Dál Fiatach

Uí Neill

Airghialla

Ui Eachach Cobha

Leth

Cathail

Connachta

Dartraige

Kingdom of the Ulaidh

Examples

Modern name in English	Irish	Meaning
Tyrone	Tír Eoghain	Land of Eoghan (or Owen).
Dalriada	Dál Riata	Riada's or Riata's share.
Fermanagh	Fir Manach	Men of Manach, (a people earlier known as the Menapii).
Keenaght	Ciannachta	Followers of Cian.
Lecale	Leth Cathail	Cathal's half (of Dál Fiatach).
Dartry	Dartraige	Calf people.
Inishowen	Inis Eoghain	Eoghan's peninsula,(literally 'island').
Larne	Latharne or Latharna	Name of a people.
Ards	Uí Eachach Arda or Aird Uladh (the peninsula of the Ulaidh)	Ards comes from **aird** meaning, in this case, a peninsula. The Uí Eachach were the descendants of Eochu who ruled here.
Iveagh	Uí Eachach Cobha	Descendants of Eochu who ruled Cobha, west Down.
Lough Neagh	Loch nEachach	Eochu's lake (the origin-legend is that King Eochu was drowned there).
Tirawley	Tír Amhlaimh	Land of Amlamh (a fourteenth-century Maguire prince in Co Fermanagh).
Mourne (Mountains)		A people pushed into these mountains by defeat in war. **Mug** means slave.

Colours

Irish words	Usual anglicisation	Meaning
bán	bane, bawn, bann	white
dubh	duff or doo	black
dearg	derg	red
ruadh	roe	red-brown
riabhach	reagh	grey
glas	glas, glass	grey/green, colour of sky
buidhe	boy, bwee	yellow
gorm	gorm	blue-black

Example	Meaning	Location
Benbane	white peak	North Antrim
Doo Lough	black lake	Fair Head
Derg river	red river	Co Tyrone
Roe river	reddish river	Co Londonderry
Castlereagh	grey castle	Belfast
Drumglass	grey/green ridge	Belfast
Derryboy	yellow oak grove	east Co Down
Gorminish	blue-black island	Co Fermanagh

NOTE: There are always exceptions which can make investigation more difficult. For example the usual anglicisation **ard** mostly means height but it can mean promontory. Ardmore means a big **height** in Co Waterford but means a big **promontory** on Lough Neagh.

Other descriptive words

Irish words	Usual anglicisation	Meaning
fionn	finn, fin	fair, beautiful
sean	shan	old
mór	more	big
beag	beg	small
fada	fad, adda, ad	long
garbh	garve, garriff, garra	rough
caol	keel	narrow
íochtar	eighter, eetra	lower
uachtar	oughter	upper
léim	leam, lem, lim	leap

Example	Meaning	Location
Fintona	fair field	Co Tyrone
Shankill	old church	Belfast
Kilmore	big church	Co Down
Ballykilbeg	townland of the small church	Co Down
Slieve Fadda	long mountain	south Co Down
Garvagh	rugged place	Co Londonderry
Ballykeel	narrow townland	Co Down
Killetra	lower wood	Co Londonderry
Lough Oughter	upper lake	Co Cavan
Limavady	dog's leap	Co Londonderry

Hill forts and promontory forts

The **dún** was almost always a king's or a noble's residence built for defence. It is a word of ancient Celtic origin; for example Lyons in France is derived from **Lugodunon**, 'the fort of Lugh'. Depending on the nature of the surrounding countryside a **dún** was built in a circular form with unmortared stone or earthen ramparts, usually with other defences. Dozens of examples could be given.

Examples

Modern name	Meaning	Location
Dunmurry	Muireadhach's fort	south Belfast/Co Antrim
Dunseverick	Sobhairce's fort	north Antrim coast
Dundonald	Donal's fort	east Belfast/Co Down
Dungannon	Ceanann's fort	east Co Tyrone
Dungiven	fort of the hide	mid Co Londonderry
Dundrum	fort of the ridge	east Co Down
Donegal	fort of the foreigners	south Co Donegal
Downpatrick	St Patrick's fort	Co Down
Down	fort	county name (from Downpatrick)

NORTHERN IRELAND TOURIST BOARD

Dungiven

Ring forts

With the exception of monastic settlements such as Armagh and Bangor, there were no real towns in Ireland until the Vikings made their home in parts of the country. People seem to have lived in isolated farmsteads as many in rural Ulster still do, and those from early and medieval times are known to historians as 'ring forts'. Between 40,000 and 60,000 ring forts have been identified and Ulster has at least its fair share of these.

Ring forts are farmsteads surrounded by a circular bank and, usually, a ditch. The ramparts may have served no more purpose than to prevent untended stock from eating the thatch off the houses. Others, however, were defensive; Congal One-Eye - the seventh-century Cruthin king of Dál nAraide and over-king of the Ulaidh - ruled from Rathmore, 'the big fort', just east of Antrim town.

In rocky or mountainous areas, where the ring fort was known as a **caiseal**, the wall was made of stone and these are commonest in Co Donegal. Where the ramparts were earthen the ring fort was called a **ráth** or a **lios**, though strictly speaking the **lios** is the inner enclosure only. The usual anglicisations are cashel, rath, and lis.

It is worth noting that houses in the Deer Park Farm rath in Glenarm, recently excavated, had cavity walls to keep out the cold.

Examples

Modern name	Meaning	Location
Cashel	stone ring fort	four places in Co Donegal, one in Co Armagh, and one in Co Londonderry
Cashelreagh	the grey fort	Co Donegal
Moygashel	plain of the fort	near Dungannon, Co Tyrone
Rathkenny	Ceannach's fort	Co Antrim
Rathmore	the big fort	south Belfast; also near Antrim
Rathfriland	Fraoile's fort	mid Co Down
Raphoe	fort of the huts	east Co Donegal; diocese name
Lisnaskea	fort of the whitethorns	Co Fermanagh
Lisnagarvey	?fort of the gamblers	former name for Lisburn
Lismore	the big fort	Co Tyrone
Lisbane	the white fort	Co Down
Lisoneill	O'Neill's fort	Co Fermanagh: where the O'Neills inaugurated Maguire chieftains

Physical features

At a time when there was only wattle-and-daub between you and the elements and when the land provided almost all food, drink, fuel and building materials, physical features assumed overwhelming importance. For example there is a wide range of words for hills of different shapes and sizes. The word **magh**, 'a plain', is common because good grazing land was prized and **tóchar**, 'a causeway', might have been vitally important to those wishing to make a quick getaway over a bog.

This list is not comprehensive but the commonest elements have been selected.

a) Words for hills and mountains

Irish words	Usual anglicisation	Meaning
beann	ben	peak
sliabh	slieve	mountain
drom	drum or drom	ridge
tulach	tully	little hill
leitir	letter	hillside
carraig	carrick	rock, often very large
carn	cairn	pile of stones on top of a hill
corr	cor, curr	round hill
craig	cregg, crag, craig	rock

cruach	croagh	hill like a corn or hay rick
duach	doagh	sand hill
éadan	eden	hill brow or slope
cnoc	knock	hill
croc (dialect variation of cnoc)	crock	hill
mullach	mullagh	crown of hill
alt	alt	height, high place
ard	ard	high, high place
aird	ard	promontory or peninsula

Examples

Modern name	Meaning	Location
Benburb	rough peak	Co Tyrone
Bangor	? place of pointed hills	Co Down
Bencrom	crooked peak	Mournes, Co Down
Binnion	little peak	Mournes, Co Down
Benmore	big peak	alternative name for Fair Head, Co Antrim
Slieve Croob	hoof mountain	mid Co Down
Slieve Donard	St Domhangart's mountain	Mournes, Co Down
Slieve Gullion	mountain of the steep unbroken slope	Co Armagh
Dromara	heifer ridge	mid Co Down
Dromore	great ridge	Co Down
Drumbo	cow ridge	north Co Down
Drumquin	pleasant ridge	Co Tyrone
Tullyhogue	little hill of the youths	O'Neill inauguration site, Co Tyrone
Tullycreevy	little hill of the branches	near Derrygonnelly, Co Fermanagh
Letterbreen	Bruin's hillside	Co Fermanagh
Lettermacaward	hillside of the Wards (sons of the Bard)	Co Donegal
Carrickmore	great rock	west Co Tyrone
Carrickfergus	Fergus's rock	Co Antrim
Carrick	rock	church in Co Fermanagh, town in Co Donegal, townland in Co Londonderry, abbey in Co Down
Carnlough	cairn of the bay	Co Antrim
Carnanbane	white cairn	Co Londonderry and Co Down
Carnaboy	yellow cairn	near Coleraine, Co Londonderry
Corralea	grey round hill	by Lough MacNean Upper, Co Fermanagh
Craigavad	rock of the boat	north Co Down
Craigy Hill	rocky hill	near Larne, Co Antrim
Cregagh	rocky place	Belfast
Croaghan	domed hill	north Co Antrim
Doagh	sand hill	south Co Antrim
Edenderry	hill brow of the oak grove	near Belfast, Co Down
Edenmore	large hill brow	Co Fermanagh and Co Down
Knock	hill	east Belfast
Knocklayd	broad hill or flat sloping hill	north Co Antrim

Crockanore	hill of gold	north Co Antrim
Mullaghnashee	hill top of the fairies	near Ballyshannon, Co Donegal
Altnagelvin	high hillside of the sparrows	Co Londonderry
Ardglass	green height	east Co Down
Ardmore	big promontory	Lough Neagh

b) Rivers, lakes, islands, inlets, wells, etc.

Irish words	Usual anglicisation	Meaning
abha, abhainn (dative case)	owen, aw, ow	river
sruth, sruthán	stra, stran (diminutive)	stream, little stream
gaoth	gwee	inlet, estuary
loch	lough	lake or sea bay
inbhear	inver	river mouth
bun	bon, bun, bunn	foot or bottom (usually of a river)
inis	inish, inch, innis, ennis	island or peninsula
ros	ross, ros	peninsula (Ulster only)
cos	cush, cosh	foot or end (usually of a river)
eas	ass, assa, ess	waterfall
eanach	anna, annagh, anny	marsh
gleann	glen	valley
cumar	comber	river joining
trá	tra, traw	strand
tobar	tober, tobber	well

Modern name	Meaning	Location
Owenreagh	grey river	Co Tyrone
Camowen	crooked river	Co Tyrone
Owenea	river of the deer	Co Donegal
Owenvarra	river of the staves (now the Blackstaff)	Belfast
Stranmillis	little sweet stream	Belfast
Strabane	white stream or white flat-bottomed river valley	Co Tyrone
Gweebarra	Barry's inlet	Co Donegal
Loughbrickland	Bricriu's lake	Co Down
Lough na Cranagh	lake of the crannóg (lake dwelling)	Fair Head, Co Antrim
Lough Foyle	sea lake or estuary	Co. Londonderry
Lough Beg	little lake	Co Londonderry and Co Antrim
Inver	river mouth	Larne and south Donegal
Bonamargy	mouth of the river Margy	north Co Antrim
Bunbeg	little river mouth	west Co Donegal
Enniskillen	Cethle's island	Co Fermanagh

Modern name	Meaning	Location
Inishowen	Eoghan's peninsula	north Co Donegal
Inishmore	big island	Co Fermanagh
Inch	island/peninsula	Co Donegal
Muckinish	pig island	Lough Erne, Co Fermanagh

Cushendall

Inishturk	boar island	Lough Erne, Co Fermanagh
Rosslea	grey peninsula (?or wood)	Co Fermanagh
Rosses	peninsulas	west Co Donegal
Cushendun	foot of the brown river	Co Antrim
Cushendall	foot of the blind river	Co Antrim
Assaroe	red waterfall	Co Fermanagh
Annaghmore	large marsh	Co Fermanagh
Glenariff	valley of the arable land	Co Antrim
Glenwhirry	valley of the whirlpool	Co Antrim
Comber	river joining	Co Down
Cultra	back of the strand	Co Down
Tobermore	big well	Co Londonderry
Tobermoney	well of the bog	near Downpatrick, Co Down

c) Other physical features

Irish words	Usual anglicisation	Meaning
áth	ath, anna	ford
cluain	clon, cloon	meadow
coill	kil, kyle	wood
cúil	col, cool, cul	nook, corner
faithche	faha, fahy, feigh	lawn, playing field
gort	gort	field
lag	lag, lig, lug	hollow
leac	lack, leck, league	flagstone
machaire	maghera, maghery	plain
magh	moy, may, ma	plain
poll	pol, poul	hole or hollow
port	fort, port	harbour, landing place
móin or monadh	mona, money	moor, peat bog, or boggy upland

Examples

Modern name	Meaning	Location
Athenry	ford of the king	near Carrickmore, Co Tyrone
Annalong	ford of the ships	Co Down
Clonard	high meadow	Belfast
Killeter	lower wood	Co Tyrone
Coole	secluded place	Co Fermanagh
Coleraine	ferny corner	Co Londonderry
Ballynafeigh	townland of the playing field	Belfast
Gortin	little field	Co Tyrone
Lagan	small hollow, low ground	Co Down and Co Antrim
Leckpatrick	St Patrick's flagstone	Co Londonderry
Maghera	plain of the ring fort	Co Down and Co Donegal
Moy	plain	Co Tyrone
Omagh	virgin or sacred plain	Co Tyrone
Pollnamona	hole of the bog	Glencolumcille, Co Donegal
Portadown	landing place of the fortress	Co Armagh
Portavogie	harbour of the bog	east Co Down
Portglenone	fort of Eoghan's meadow	Co Antrim
Moneymore	large bog	Co Londonderry

Trees

Irish words	Usual anglicisation	Meaning
beith	beagh, behy, vehy	birch
cuileann	cullen, gullion	holly (but can mean steep unbroken slope)
daire or doire	der, derry	oak wood
draighean	dreen, drain, drin	blackthorn
saileach	sallagh, sillagh	sallow, or willow
fearn	fern, farn	alder
fuinse	funshin, funcheon	ash
iubhar, iúr	ure	yew
leamhán	levan, livan, lamph	elm, little elm
sceach	skeagh, skea	whitethorn
trom	trim, trom, trum	elder
coll	coll, cull, coyle, kyle	hazel
fiodh	fews, feigh, feth	wood
crann	cran	tree
craobh	creeve, creevy	branch or branchy tree

Examples

Modern name	Meaning	Location
Glenveagh	glen of birches	Co Donegal
Glenhull	valley of hazel	Co Tyrone
Derrygonnelly	oak grove of the O'Connollys	Co Fermanagh
Ballysallagh	townland of the willows	near Bangor, Co Down
Farney	plain of the alders	Co Monaghan
Ballynure	townland of the yew	south Co Armagh
Newry	yew tree or yew tree at the head of strand	Co Down

Lisnaskea	ring fort of the whitethorns	Co Fermanagh
Fews	woods	south Co Armagh
Creevagh More	big branchy place	near Ballycastle, Co Antrim

Houses

Irish words	Usual anglicisation	Meaning
tigh, or teach	tee, ti, ta	house
tor	tor	mansion or tower
badhún	bawn	fortified enclosure
brugh	brough	palace or fairy house
cloch	clough, clogh	stone castle

NORTHERN IRELAND TOURIST BOARD

Torr Head

Examples

Modern name	Meaning	Location
Bawnmore	large enclosure	Belfast
Broughshane	Shane's palace	Co Antrim
Clough	castle made of stone	Co Down

Townlands, towns and land divisions

Irish words	Usual anglicisation	Meaning
baile	bally, ballin, bal	townland or town
ceathramhadh	carrow, carry, kerry	quarter (usually of a townland)
séisíoch	sessiagh	sixth (usually of a townland)
trian	rin, erin	third (usually of a kingdom)
ceapach	cap, cappa, cappagh	plot of land laid out for tillage
buaile	boley, booley, bola	summer pasture

Examples

Modern name	Meaning	Location
Ballycarry	townland of the weir	east Co Antrim
Ballygawley	O'Daly's townland	Co Tyrone
Ballymena	middle town	Co Antrim
Ballykelly	O'Kelly's townland	Co Londonderry
Carryduff	black Hugh's quarter	north Co Down
Carrowdore	quarter of the water	east Co Down
Sessiagh	sixth	north Co Donegal
Sessiadonaghy	O'Donaghy's sixth	near Dungannon, Co Tyrone
Dufferin	black third	Co Down
Cappagh	land cleared of wood for tillage	near Dungannon, Co Tyrone
Ballyboley	townland of the summer pasture	Co Antrim

The word 'townland', used as a translation of **baile,** can be misleading because it was a division of land, usually with no town at all, which varied in size according to the fertility of the soil or the number of cattle which could be grazed on it. Today **baile** simply means 'town'.

Religion and the Church

Oak groves were of great importance to the pagan Irish and it is particularly in Ulster that the word 'derry' - from **doire**, meaning an oak grove - appears in place names. Some of these places became Christian sites. The Irish were conservation minded and did not destroy portal tombs and other prehistoric monuments, often marked in place names beginning with 'leg', from **liag,** meaning a monument stone.

For many centuries the Church was the centre of wealth and learning, and the pioneer in town building and agricultural improvement. It therefore had a major impact on place names. Many words associated with the Church are Latin in origin.

Irish words	Usual anglicisation	Meaning
doire	derry, derra	oak grove
liag	leg, legaun	stone monument
cill	kil, kill, or killy	church
aireagal	errigal	a cell or oratory
domhnach	don, donagh, dun, doney	large church (early)
díseart	desert, disert, dysert	hermitage
teampall	temple, tempal	church (medieval)
tamlacht	tamlaght, tallaght	burying ground
leaba	labba, labby	portal tomb or bed (meaning grave)
tearmann	termon	church land, sanctuary
sagart	saggart, taggart	priest
cros	cross, crosh, crush	cross or cross roads

Examples

Modern name	Meaning	Location
Kilbroney	church of St Bronach	Co Down
Killadeas	church of the Culdees (church reformers)	near Enniskillen, Co Fermanagh
Killinchy	church of St Duinseach	Co Down
Kilrea	russet church	Co Londonderry

Londonderry

Killough	church of the bay	Strangford Lough, Co Down
Killybegs	small churches	Co Donegal
Derry	oak grove	Derry City/London-derry
Ballinderry	townland of the oak grove	Co Londonderry
Legananny	stone monument of the marsh	portal tomb, Co Down
Errigal	oratory	mountain in Co Donegal
Errigal Keeroge	oratory of St Dachiarog	near Augher, Co Tyrone
Crossmaglen	cross of the son of Lionnan	south Co Armagh
Donaghmore	large church	near Dungannon, Co Tyrone
Donaghcloney	church of the meadow	Co Down
Kilnasaggart	church of the priests	Co Armagh
Termon river	sanctuary river	Fermanagh and Donegal border
Termon MacGrath	sanctuary or church land of the MacGraths	Lough Erne
Templepatrick	St Patrick's church	Co Antrim
Desertmartin	St Martin's hermitage	Co Londonderry
Tamlaght	graveyard	near Swatragh, Co Londonderry
Tamlaghtard	high graveyard	near Limavady, Co Londonderry
Labby Dermot	Dermot's grave	near Carrickmore, Co Tyrone
Labby	grave	Co Donegal

Viking place names

The Vikings began their raids on Ulster at the end of the eighth century and during periods of the ninth and tenth centuries they plundered inland to Armagh and had fleets on Lough Neagh and Lough Erne. Yet they found Ulster difficult to conquer and concentrated their colonisation in Dublin, Waterford, Limerick and other southern coastlands.

The only lasting Viking settlements seem to have been at Larne and Strangford, and this list below is probably a complete list of Viking names in Ulster.

Modern name	Meaning	Location
Carlingford	the carlin's or hag's fjord	south-east Ulster
Olderfleet	a corruption of 'Ulfrek's fjord', Larne Lough	Co Antrim
Strangford	strong inlet: tide race at mouth of lough	Co Down
Skerries	from Old Norse meaning rocks	Portrush, Co Antrim
Ulster	Viking adaptation of Irish words **tír** (land) of the **Ulaidh**, which in their spelling became **Uladztír**	northern province

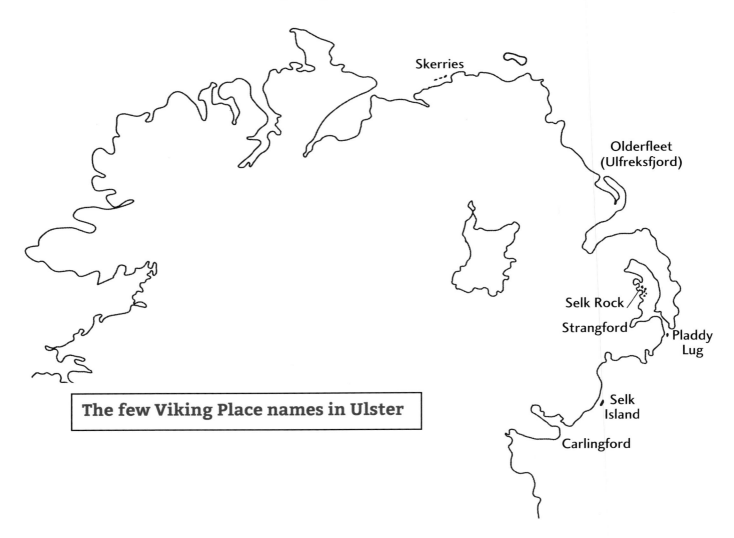

Skerries

Olderfleet
(Ulfreksfjord)

Selk Rock

Strangford

Pladdy
Lug

Selk
Island

Carlingford

The few Viking Place names in Ulster

Modern name	Meaning	Location
* Selk Island	seal island	near Annalong, Co Down
* Selk Rock	seal rock	near Killyleagh, Co Down
* Pladdy	flat island	off Ballyquintin Point, Co Down

*almost certainly named by Scots settlers in the seventeenth century; **selk** and **pladdy** are both Lowland Scots dialect words of Danish or Norse origin.

Anglo-Norman place names

The Normans conquered much of east Down and south Antrim fairly rapidly at the end of the twelfth century. Later they extended their rule up the Glens, around north Antrim to north Derry and even for a time to Inishowen. But Ulster was always a dangerous marchland on the edge of the English Lordship in Ireland and the conquerors could not attract the same number of settlers as they did to north Leinster. Names from the medieval period ending in - **ton** or - **town** are a good indication of heavy Anglo-Norman settlement. These abound in parts of Leinster but are rare in Ulster. Thirteenth-century inquisitions show the names the Anglo-Normans gave to their towns and manors. Many of those simply used the native Irish place names.

Dun (Downpatrick); **Blathewyc** (Newtownards); **Dunmalys** (Larne) **Wulfricksford** (Olderfleet); **Portkamen** (Bushmills); **Portros** (Portrush); **Grenecastell** (Greencastle); **Doundannald** (Dundonald); **Coul** (Carnmoney); **Le Ford** (Belfast); **Twywys** (Ballynure); **Lyn** (the Cutts); **Coulrath** (Coleraine); **del Art** (Ards); **Ladcathel** (Lecale); **Northburgh** (Greencastle, Co Donegal); **Twescard** (from **tuaisceart**, meaning 'north' in Irish, around Bushmills); **le Roo** (Limavady); **Talbotiston** (Ballyhalbert); the manors of **Robertiston** and **Waltirton** in the Six Mile Water valley; and **Halywode** (Holywood).

Greencastle, County Donegal

The Normans built motte-and-bailey castles and stone castles to maintain a hold on the Earldom of Ulster. The most permanent settlements were at Carrickfergus, the Ards peninsula and Lecale. Why did the Anglo-Norman place names not stick? The answer is that except for Carrickfergus the Irish overwhelmed the colony in the late fourteenth and fifteenth centuries. Only a few place names survived.

Carrickfergus Castle

Examples

Modern name	Meaning	Location
Holywood	a translation of its medieval Latin name SANCTUM BOSCUM	north Co Down
Ballyhalbert	a part Gaelicisation of 'Talbot's town'	Ards peninsula
Ballywalter	'Walter's town'	Ards peninsula
Ballywalter and Ballyrobert	Gaelicisation of 'Walter's town' and 'Robert's town'	Six Mile Water townlands, Co Antrim
Greencastle	name for Hugh de Lacy's castle	south Co Down
Greencastle	name for Richard de Burgh's castle	Inishowen, Co Donegal
Greyabbey	founded by Affreca de Courcy	Ards peninsula
Audley's castle	fifteenth-century tower house	Co Down
Jordan's castle	fifteenth-century tower house	Co Down

Anglo-Norman Ulster

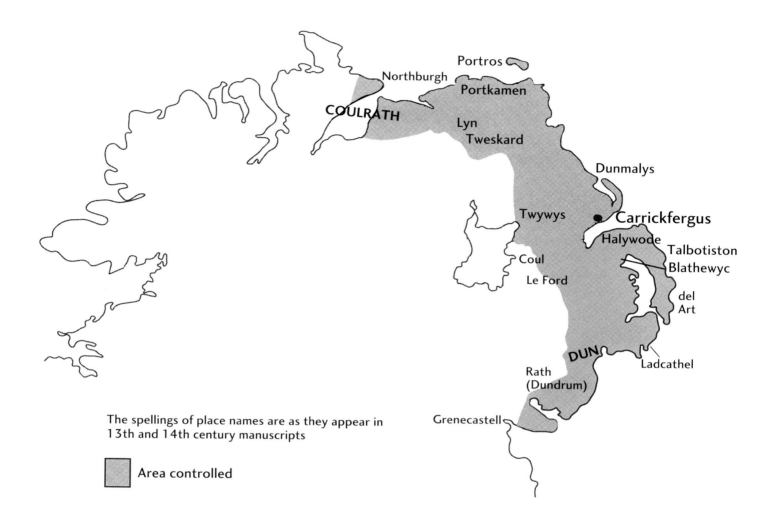

Portros

Northburgh

Portkamen

COULRATH

Lyn
Tweskard

Dunmalys

Twywys

Carrickfergus

Halywode

Talbotiston

Coul

Blathewyc

Le Ford

del
Art

DUN

Rath
(Dundrum)

Ladcathel

Grenecastell

The spellings of place names are as they appear in
13th and 14th century manuscripts

Area controlled

The Anglo-Normans often used local Irish names for their castles.

Examples

Modern name	Meaning	Location
Carrickfergus	Fergus's rock	Belfast Lough
Dundrum	fort on the ridge	east Co Down
Clough	stone or stone building	east Co Down
Dromore	big ridge	north Co Down
Antrim	? one tribe ? elder tree	Co Antrim
Ballyroney	O'Rooney's townland	Co Down
Coleraine	ferny corner	Co Londonderry
Donegore	fort of the goats	south Co Antrim
Dundonald	Donal's fort	north Co Down
Seafin	Fionn's seat	west Co Down
Doonbought	poor fort	mid Co Antrim

NORTHERN IRELAND TOURIST BOARD

Enniskillen

From the mid-fourteenth century, but especially in the fifteenth and sixteenth centuries, the Irish and Gaelic Scots built many castles across Ulster.

Examples

Modern name	Meaning	Location	Main owners
'Harry Avery's Castle'	Henrí Aimhréidh O'Neill's castle	west Co Tyrone	(Sliocht Henrí) O'Neill
Dunluce	fort	north Co Antrim	MacQuillans, then rebuilt by MacDonnells
Donegal	fort of the foreigners	south Co Donegal	O'Donnells
Dunseverick	Sobhairce's fort	north Co Antrim	O'Cahans
Belfast	approach to the sandbank	Belfast	Clandeboye O'Neills
Castlereagh	grey castle	south Belfast	Clandeboye O'Neills
Omagh	sacred plain	Co Tyrone	(Sliocht Airt) O'Neills
Doe	from MacSuibhne na dTuath, ie MacSweeny of the Tribes (castle of MacSweeny na Doe)	north Co Donegal	MacSweenys (northern branch)
Enniskillen	Cethle's island	Co Fermanagh	Maguires
Newcastle	new castle	Co Down	Magennises
Benburb	rough peak	south Co Tyrone	O'Neills
'Shanes Castle' (then known as Edenduffcarrick)	named after Shane O'Neill / the black face of the rock	north Lough Neagh	Clandeboye O'Neills
Portaferry	harbour of the ferry	east Co Down	Savages

Places named in English

Apart from the few medieval Norman names, the vast majority in Ulster date from the Plantation onwards, that is, from the early seventeenth century. The official Plantation - colonisation by Protestant English and Lowland Scots - covered the counties of Armagh, Tyrone, Fermanagh, Cavan, Donegal (formerly Tyrconnell) and Londonderry (formerly Coleraine). Large grants of land in the counties of Antrim and Down were made to soldiers and favourites by King James I and the colonisation here was more successful than elsewhere in the province.

Almost all the newcomers spoke English, though in a wide variety of dialects including Lowland Scots. Even where they greatly outnumbered the native Irish they usually retained the local Irish place names but came to pronounce and spell those names in their own way. The distribution of place names in English is some guide to the success or failure of colonisation - for example, there are many more English-language place names in Co Down than in Co Tyrone.

A high proportion of place names in English are named after leading settler families or coined by them. In some places old Irish names were given English equivalents or alternatives.

Examples

Irish name (anglicised)	Meaning	New name	Location
Ben Madigan	Madigan's peak	Cave Hill	north Belfast
Ben More	big peak	Fair Head	north Co Antrim
Owenvarra	river of staves	Blackstaff	Belfast
Ben Gorm	blue peak	Bluestack mountains	Co Donegal
Muff	the plain	Eglinton	near Derry City

The Elizabethan conquest

At the start of Elizabeth I's reign only Carrickfergus and Newry (then called 'The Newry' from the Irish **Iubhar Cinn Tragha**, 'yew tree at the head of the strand') were firmly in English hands and it took a major war (1594-1603) to conquer the province from end to end. During this conflict several forts were built, some of which became towns.

Examples

Modern name	Meaning	Location
Blackwatertown	built 1597; attempt by Marshal Henry Bagenal to relieve it led to defeat of English at Yellow Ford 1598	north of Armagh city
Mountnorris	built 1601 and named after Sir John Norris	north west of Newry
Mountjoy	built 1603 and named after English commander	south east corner Lough Neagh
Charlemont	built 1603 and named from Charles Blount, Lord Mountjoy	north Co Armagh

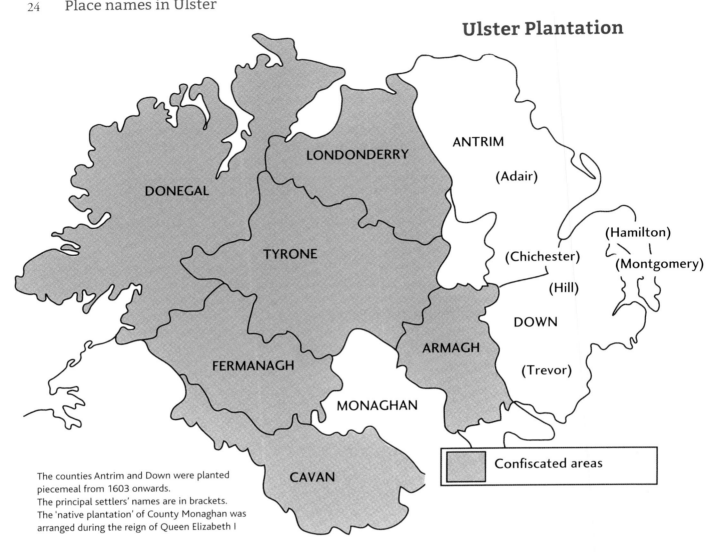

Ulster Plantation

Confiscated areas

The counties Antrim and Down were planted piecemeal from 1603 onwards.
The principal settlers' names are in brackets.
The 'native plantation' of County Monaghan was arranged during the reign of Queen Elizabeth I

Landowners

In 1607 the Earl of Tyrone, the Earl of Tyrconnell, Lord Maguire and about a hundred other members of the Gaelic nobility of Ulster left Ireland for ever. The English government decided that this was unlawful and confiscated their lands, especially after Sir Cahir O'Doherty's burning of Derry in 1609. The 'Plantation of Ulster' got under way in 1610. Land was given to 'servitors' (who had served as officers and civil servants), 'undertakers' (who undertook to colonise the land) and 'deserving Irish' (who had stayed loyal to the government). The biggest undertaker was the City of London merchant corporation which was given the county of Coleraine, which with additions became Co Londonderry.

Not as many places are named after these planters as might be expected. Estates were granted to these planters under the Irish townland names. Some colonists never turned up, some sold out to others, and many were happy to keep the Irish place names there already. Further confiscations in the 1650s brought in many new owners. Often land agents and tenants became as important as the original owners.

Meanwhile large areas of Down and Antrim had been granted by James I to Sir Arthur Chichester , the viceroy, and two Scottish lairds - Hugh Montgomery and Hugh Hamilton. The colonisation of Antrim and Down was more successful than the official 'Plantation of Ulster.'

NORTHERN IRELAND TOURIST BOARD

Hillsborough

Examples

Modern name	Meaning	Location
Hillsborough Hilltown Hillhall Church Hill	north Co Down south Co Down near Lisburn north Co Donegal, named by Lord George Hill in 19th century	Sir Moses Hill, a soldier of Elizabeth I, was a tenant of Sir Arthur Chichester. Later descendants became the Marquesses of Downshire
Mountstewart	Ards peninsula	From Scots settlers in Donegal. Alexander Stewart, son of Col.W. Stewart, bought Co Down estates with his wife's fortune.
Brookeborough	east Co Fermanagh	Founded by descendants of Sir Basil Brooke, servitor who settled south Donegal. Got Fermanagh estate after owner Lord Maguire was hanged in 1641.
Colebrooke	east Co Fermanagh	The Brookes were from Cheshire. Sir William Cole got Enniskillen as a servitor but his family male line ran out. A marriage between the two families in 1652 created this estate and town.
Castleblaney	Co Monaghan	Founded by the servitor Sir Edward Blaney.
Castlecaldwell	Co Fermanagh	Founded by Francis Blennerhasset in 1612 but sold to James Caldwell in 1662.

Castlecaulfield	east Co Tyrone	The servitor, Sir Toby Caulfield, built a mansion here in 1614. Ancestor of Earls of Charlemont.
Cootehill	Co Cavan	Founded by a notable soldier of the 1640s.
Waringstown	west Co Down	Founded by English merchant family which made its fortune in hides and tanning. Also named Waring St. in Belfast.
Seaforde	east Co Down	Founded by the Fordes of Co Wexford, a family of Welsh origin. Still there today.
Castleward	south-east Co Down	Estate of the Ward family, English settlers (?from Suffolk).
Crawfordsburn	near Bangor, Co Down	From Lanarkshire settlers, tenants of Hamiltons who built Bangor.
Newtowncunningham Manorcunningham	north Donegal	Founded and named from two Ulster Plantation grantees from Ayrshire and Wigtownshire.
Rutland Island	off Burtonport, west Donegal	Named by a Duke of Rutland who spent £40,000 in the 18th century developing the herring industry here.
Maguire's Bridge	Co Fermanagh	Named from Lord Maguire, a 'deserving native', who rebelled in 1641 and then was hanged. Estates confiscated.
Castle Archdale	Co Fermanagh	Named by a grantee of Ulster Plantation who came from Suffolk
Salterstown	western shore Lough Neagh	Unsuccessful Plantation town founded by the London company of Salters.
Draperstown	south-east Co Londonderry	Founded by the London Company of Drapers.
Baronscourt	north Co Tyrone	Founded by a Baron Hamilton, ancestor of the Dukes of Abercorn.

Randalstown	west Co Antrim	Named after the 'deserving native' Sir Randal MacDonnell, who could also claim to be a Scot.
Newtownhamilton	south Co Armagh	Founded 1770 by a local Hamilton landlord.
Hamilton's Bawn	South Co Armagh	From a fortification built by a John Hamilton, an Ulster Plantation grantee from East Lothian.
Cookstown	Co. Tyrone	Granted to Allan Cook in the Plantation, but built by William Stewart MP in 1736.

NORTHERN IRELAND TOURIST BOARD

Castle Ward, County Down

Further examples of places named after landowners are listed below

Modern name	Location
Newtownbutler	Co Fermanagh
Stewartstown	Co Tyrone
Irvinestown	Co Fermanagh
Poyntzpass	Co Armagh
Richill	Co Armagh
Bryansford	Co Down
Portstewart	Co Londonderry
Castlesaunderson	Co Fermanagh
Newtownstewart	Co Tyrone
Rostrevor	Co Down
Smithborough	Co Monaghan
Rankinstown	Co Antrim
Castledawson	Co Londonderry
Grahamstown	Co Tyrone

Other place names in English

Examples

Modern name	Location and comment
Rabbit, Owl, White, Heron, Duck, Goat, Loftus, Bingham, Black, Long, The Spike, Gravel Ridge,	Lower Lough Erne: all of these are islands and rocks. In fact, there are two White islands.
Maggy's Leap, Mullartown Point, Long Point, Crawford's Point, Nicholson's Point, Soldier's Point	Headlands between Newcastle along the Mourne coast round to Greencastle in Co Down.
Walkmills	Co Antrim: where weavers 'walked' in tubs to clean the woollen cloth.
Whiteside's Corner	near Ballymena, Co Antrim
Agnew's Hill	near Larne, Co Antrim
Hunter's Point	near Carnlough, Co Antrim
Eagle Hill	close to Trostan, Antrim Plateau
Church Bay	Rathlin Island, Co Antrim
White Rocks and Black Rocks	on either side of Portrush, Co Antrim
Wreck Port, Samuel's Port, Green Harbour	Bays near Annalong, Co Down
Fivemiletown	Co Tyrone
Six Mile Cross	Co Tyrone
Six Road Ends	between Newtownards and Donaghadee, Co Down
Molly Blaney's Corner	south east of Downpatrick, Co Down
Cross Keys; The Flying Horse; Blackskull	landmarks named from taverns: Co Antrim and Co Down
May's Corner	near Ballyroney, Co Down
Eliza Hill	near Banbridge, Co Down
The Sheddings	watershed at headwaters Braid river, Co Antrim
Black Causeway	near Strangford, Co Down

NORTHERN IRELAND TOURIST BOARD

The Crosskeys Inn, County Antrim

Street names: examples from Belfast

Sir Arthur Chichester was a leading commander during the final subjugation of Gaelic Ulster at the close of Elizabeth I's reign. He was granted Belfast and much else besides in 1603 and later acquired Inishowen in north Donegal. Appointed Lord Deputy in 1605, Chichester was in charge of the Plantation of Ulster and he was therefore determined to set a good example in Belfast. His successors were the Earls of Donegall (so named because of the Inishowen acquisition) and until George Augustus Chichester, the second Marquis, blew the family fortune on horses and women at the beginning of the nineteenth century, virtually all of the town was owned by the Chichesters. Not surprisingly many streets are named after members of the family. For example: Donegall Street; Donegall Place; Donegall Road; Donegall Pass; Donegall Avenue; Donegall Quay; Donegall Park; Donegall Park Avenue; Donegall Square; Donegall Parade; Arthur Street; Chichester Avenue; Chichester Close; Chichester Park; Chichester Gardens; Chichester Street; Alfred Street; Rosemary Street; Howard Street; and Ann Street. Squire's Hill is named after the first Sir Arthur's agent; Oldpark was once the family deer park. May Street and May's Markets were named after the second Marquis's wife's family.

Yet many of the Irish names were retained for different districts engulfed by the town in the nineteenth century (then the fastest-growing urban centre in the United Kingdom). For example: Malone ('plain of provisions'); Falls ('enclosed area'); Shankill ('old church'). Stranmillis ('sweet little stream'); Cromac ('the bending'), where the Blackstaff curved as it flowed into the Lagan ('river hollow');

NORTHERN IRELAND TOURIST BOARD

Belfast city centre

Ardoyne ('Eoghan's height'); Divis ('black peak'); Poleglass ('green hole'); Ligoneill ('hollow of limestone'); Ballymacarrett ('MacGarrett's townland'); Ballylesson ('townland of the little fort'); Gilnahirk ('gillie of the horn'); Knock ('hill'), Ballynafeigh ('townland of the playing field'); Cregagh ('rocky place'); Finaghy ('white field'); Galwally ('territory of the foreigners'); Ballygomartin ('townland of Martin's enclosure'). All of these places have streets named from them.

The Belfast Corporation was one of the most energetic town councils in the United Kingdom in the mid-nineteenth century. It built many streets choosing names that proclaimed its loyalty to the Crown: for example Corporation Street, intended to be the main thoroughfare of Belfast; Victoria Square; Great Victoria Street; and Royal Avenue (not built until the 1880s to replace Hercules Street).

High Street had been the main street in the seventeenth and eighteenth centuries. The river Farset which ran down the middle was covered over in the 1770s. Leading off High Street were 'entries' such as Joy's Entry (named after the founder of the 'Belfast News Letter', Francis Joy), Pottinger's Entry (named after a politician and merchant from Ballymacarrett) and Crown Entry.

Waring Street (after a seventeenth-century entrepreneur); North Street (because it led out of the North Gate when Belfast had ramparts); Linen Hall Street (because it led from the Linen Hall, built in the 1780s and pulled down in the 1890s to make way for the City Hall); Fountain Street (an early water source); and College Square (after "Inst"- Royal Belfast Academical Institution).

Most of the side streets and housing estates were built by private developers. Linen lords put up cheap housing for rent near their mills (these, for the most part, have mercifully been swept away) and later, when the Corporation had bye-laws insisting on back entries and other minimum standards - building firms and estate agents put up terrace, 'kitchen' and suburban housing for skilled workers and the middle classes. The chosen street names tend to appears in clusters. 'The Holy Land', built on the 'Plains' near Stranmillis: Jerusalem Street; Carmel Street; Damascus Street; and Cairo Street. 'Sailorstown' in north central Belfast: Nelson Street; Marine Street; Dock Street; Ship Street; and many others swept away to clear the approaches to the M2. Many streets off the Oldpark Road were named after rivers - such as Shannon Street, Liffey Street and Roe Street - but most have been knocked down. First World War streets off the Cregagh Road: Thiepval Avenue; Bapaume Avenue; Picardy Avenue; Albert Drive; Hamel Drive; and Somme Drive. Streets named after viceroys off the Lisburn Road such as Camden Street; Fitzwilliam Street; Wellesley Avenue; and Wellington Park.

New names are being coined every year by the D.O.E. (notably, the West Link ring road), by the Housing Executive (in Poleglass, for example) and by developers (Thornhill Malone, for example).

TELEGRAMS, PORTWILLIAM.

MONREITH.
WHAUPHILL,
WIGTOWNSHIRE.

9 October 1924

Dear Lady Londonderry

Lord knows where you are by this time, but I will address this to Mount Stewart on the chance of hitting you in your orbit. I am much amused by your taking up Gaelic place names. I do not know of any dictionary that gives the English sound of Gaelic names; the book for your purpose (if you pursue the study) is the Origin and History of Irish Names of Places, 3 vols, by Dr Joyce, published by McGill and Son, Dublin. He gives the English pronunciation of every name. Irish and Scots Gaelic, as you well know, are one language, only differing from each other in similar measure as Clydesdale English differs from Cornish. In both Irish and Scots Gaelic the orthography is most perplexing,

PRONI. D3099/3/19/1/7

Further investigation

The great pioneer study, as the excerpt above makes clear, is **The Origin and History of Irish Names of Places** by P.W. Joyce. The first volume appeared in 1869 and it is an indication of Joyce's scholarship that modern experts still accept about two thirds of his definitions. Popular works still tend to draw almost exclusively on Joyce. They include **The AA Book of Ireland, The Shell Guide to Ireland** (but not the latest edition) and **The Meaning of Irish Place Names** by James O'Connell. (Blackstaff) 1978.

Much important revision of Joyce has been carried out and this is succinctly summarised by Deirdre Flanagan, **Supplement for Schools (Bulletin of the Ulster Place-Name Society** ser. II vol. 4 1981-2) which includes 'Some Guidelines To The Use of Joyce's Irish Names of Places. Volume I'. Deirdre Flanagan points out the errors in O'Connell's book in a review (**BUPNS ser II vol. 2**). Deirdre Flanagan's Supplement for Schools (see above) includes a very full bibliography on pages 67-69; see also her article **Ulster Local Studies** vol. II No 1. (1976).

In short, the best way to keep up-to-date with latest research is to consult **The Bulletin of the Ulster Place-Name Society,** now called **Ainm,** published by the Celtic Department, Queen's University Belfast, and also publications of the Place-Name Project as they appear.

There are no short guides to Anglo-Norman and English place names in Ulster. Works of value include: W. Reeves, **Ecclesiastical Antiquities of Down, Connor and Dromore** (1847); G.H. Orpen, 'The Earldom of Ulster" in **the Journal of the Royal Society of Antiquaries (Ireland)** 1913, 1914 and 1915; T.E. McNeill, **Anglo-Norman Ulster** (1980); Philip Robinson, **The Plantation of Ulster** (1984); Cyril Falls, **Elizabeth's Irish Wars** (1950); and town and county histories, Ordnance Survey Memoirs, and numerous other local histories. See also **Eire Thuaidh** (Ordnance Survey 1988), a large detailed map of Ireland with place names in Irish - very helpful to any class investigating Ulster place names.

Schools preparing for field trips or a classroom project would find the **six-inch maps** (Ordnance Survey and Public Records Office) and **Local Government District Townland index maps** (Ordnance Survey 1974) invaluable. A comparison of early and modern maps of the same area would also be rewarding. Maps of the Plantation can be seen in the Public Record Office at Balmoral Avenue in Belfast: consult **T 1652 Escheated County Maps**. Sir William Petty was the great map maker in the later seventeenth century. His barony maps may be found in larger libaries (known as the **Down Survey**) but his **Hiberniae Delineatio**, with an introduction by J.H. Andrews, was printed by Shannon Press in 1969 and should be more widely available.

Those who can read and understand Irish could consult **Ainmneacha Gaeilge na mBailte Poist** (1969) and **Gasaitéar na hEireann** (1990), published by the Ordnance Survey of Ireland, Phoenix Park, Dublin. The **Ordnance Survey Memoirs,** detailed descriptions of parishes in Ulster in the 1830's and 1840's provide excellent classroom material not only for history teachers but also for investigating place names. These are being published in several inexpensive volumes by the Institute of Irish studies. Extracts from these memoirs have been edited for school use in John Dooher's publication, **Living and Working in Pre-Famine Ulster**, Northern Ireland Centre for Learning Resources (1991).

A brief but highly-informative article, which discusses the problems encountered in investigating place names, is **The Place-Name Research Project, Queen's University, Belfast** by Kay Muhr and is found in chapter 14 of **Aspects of Irish Studies**, edited by Myrtle Hill and Sarah Barber, (Institute of Irish Studies Q.U.B. 1990). This chapter includes an extract from Petty's **Political Anatomy of Ireland:**

"Ireland is now divided into provinces, counties, baronies, parishes and farmlands...but formerly it was not so, but the country was called by the names of the lords who governed the people. For as a territory bounded by bogs is greater or lesser as the bog is more dry and passable, or otherwise: so the country of a grandee or tierne in Ireland became greater or lesser as his forces waxed or waned...And when these grandees came to make peace and parts one with another, the limits of their land agreements were no lines geometrically drawn, but if the rain fell one way then the land whereon it fell did belong to A, if the other way to B, etc. As to their town lands, plow-lands, colps, gneeves, bullibos, ballibetaghs...etc., they are all at this day become unequal both in quantity and value, having been drawn upon grounds which were obsolete and antiquated...But now all the lands are geometrically divided, and that without abolishing the ancient denominations and divisions above mentioned..."

Index

Jonathan Bardon: a select bibliography

A Narrow Sea: The Irish-Scottish Connection in 120 Episodes (Dublin: Gill Books, 2018).
Hallelujah: The Story of a Musical Genius and the City that Brought His Masterpiece to Life (Dublin: Gill & Macmillan, 2015).
Ulster and the First World War (Belfast: Northern Ireland War Memorial, 2014).
From GI Brides to the Modern Family: 65 years of Relate NI (Belfast: Relate Northern Ireland, 2014).
The Plantation of Ulster: The British Colonisation of the North of Ireland in the Seventeenth Century (Dublin: Gill & Macmillan, 2011).
The Struggle for Shared Schools in Northern Ireland: The History of All Children Together (Belfast: Ulster Historical Foundation, 2010).
A History of Ireland in 250 Episodes (Dublin: Gill & Macmillan, 2008).
The 1608 Royal Schools Celebrate 400 years of History, 1608–2008 (Northern Ireland: 1608 Royal Schools, 2007).
An Interesting and Honourable History: The Belfast Charitable Society. The First 250 Years, 1752–2002 (Belfast: Belfast Charitable Society, 2003).
A Guide to Local History Sources in the Public Record Office of Northern Ireland (Belfast: Blackstaff, 2000).
Beyond the Studio: A History of BBC Northern Ireland (Belfast: Blackstaff, 2000).
Belfast: A Century (Belfast: Blackstaff, 1999).
A Shorter Illustrated History of Ulster (Belfast: Blackstaff, 1996).
A History of Ulster (Belfast: Blackstaff Press, 1992).
Belfast: 1000 years (Belfast: Blackstaff, 1985).
Dublin: One Thousand Years of Wood Quay (Belfast: Blackstaff, 1984).
Belfast: An Illustrated History (Dundonald: Blackstaff, *c.* 1982).
The Struggle for Ireland, 400 AD–1450 AD (Belfast: Fallons, 1970).

Further reading

Books

F. H. A., Aalen, Kevin Whelan and Matthew Stout (eds), *Atlas of the Irish Rural Landscape* (Cork: Cork University Press, 1997).

J. H. Andrews, *A Paper Landscape: The Ordnance Survey in Nineteenth-Century Ireland* (Oxford: Clarendon Press, 1975).

—, *Plantation Acres: An Historical Study of the Irish Land Surveyor and his Maps* (Belfast: Ulster Historical Foundation, 1985).

—, *Shapes of Ireland: Maps and Their Makers 1564–1839* (Dublin: Geography Publications, 1997).

—, *The Queen's Last Map-Maker: Richard Bartlett in Ireland, 1600–3* (Dublin: Geography Publications, 2008).

Patricia Boyne, *John O'Donovan (1806–1861): A Biography* (Kilkenny: Boethius Press, 1987).

Eve Campbell, *The Field Names of County Louth* (Drogheda: Louth Field Names Project, 2014).

Charles Close, *The Early Years of the Ordnance Survey* (Newtown Abbot: David & Charles, 1969).

T. F. Colby, *Ordnance Survey of the County of Londonderry: Memoir of the City and North-Western Liberties of Londonderry, Parish of Templemore* (Dublin: Hodges and Smith for H. M. Government, 1837).

W. H. Crawford and R. H. Foy, *Townlands in Ulster: Local History Studies* (Belfast: Ulster Historical Foundation, 1998).

Angélique Day, *Glimpses of Ireland's Past: the Ordnance Survey Memoir Drawings: Topography and Technique* (Dublin: Royal Irish Academy, 2014).

Gillian Doherty, *The Irish Ordnance Survey: History, Culture and Memory* (Dublin: Four Courts Press, 2004).

Bernadette Donnelly (ed.), *South Lough Neagh: 'Skimming the Surface'* (Dungannon: South Lough Neagh Publishing, 2005).

P. J. Duffy, *Landscapes of South Ulster: A Parish Atlas of the Diocese of Clogher* (Belfast: Institute of Irish Studies, QUB, 1993).

Deirdre and Laurence Flanagan, *Irish Place Names* (Dublin: Gill & Macmillan, 1994).

Brian Friel, *Translations* (London: Faber and Faber Ltd, 1981).

Pat Grimes, *Muintirevlin Remembers: The History of the People Around the Old Cross* (Cookstown: Muintirevlin Historical Society, 2000).

Michael Herity (ed.), *Ordnance Survey Letters Donegal: Letters Containing Information Relative to the Antiquities of the County of Donegal Collected During the Progress of the Ordnance Survey in 1835* (Dublin: Four Masters Press, 2000).

— (ed.), *Ordnance Survey Letters Down: Letters Containing Information Relative to the Antiquities of the County of Down Collected During the Progress of the Ordnance Survey in 1834* (Dublin: Four Masters Press, 2001). Other publications on the Ordnance Survey Letters (ed.) Michael Herity.

Rachel Hewitt, *Map of a Nation: A Biography of the Ordnance Survey* (London: Granta, 2010).

E. I. Hogan, *Onomasticon Goedelicum: An Index, with Identifications, to the Gaelic Names of Places and Tribes* (Dublin: Hodges Figgis, 1910). Online at University College Cork: http://research.ucc.ie/doi/locus.

T. E. Jordan, *An Imaginative Empiricist: Thomas Aiskew Larcom (1801–1879) and Victorian Ireland* (Lewiston NY: Mellon Press, 2002).

P. W. Joyce, *The Origin and History of Irish Names of Places*, 3 vols (Dublin: Gill and Son/The Educational Co. of Ireland Ltd, 1910–120). Available on the website of Ask About Ireland (www.askaboutireland.ie).

Richard Kirwan, *If Maps Could Speak* (Dublin: Londubh Books, 2010).

Patrick McKay, *A Dictionary of Ulster Place-Names* (Belfast: Institute of Irish Studies, QUB, 1999, 2nd ed. 2007).

Patrick McKay and Kay Muhr, *Lough Neagh Places: Their Names and Origins*, (Belfast: Cló Ollscoil na Banríona, Belfast, 2007).

Graham Mawhinney (ed.), *John O'Donovan's Letters from County Londonderry* (1834) (Draperstown, Co. Londonderry: Ballinascreen Historical Society, 1992).

Kay Muhr, *Celebrating Ulster's Townlands* (Belfast: Ulster-Place Names Society, 1999). An A4 booklet (32 pp) to accompany the Ulster Place-Name Society travelling exhibition for the Millennium. (www.ulsterplacename.org).

Joan Mullen and Frances Tallon, *The Field Names of County Meath* (Drogheda: The Meath Field Names Project, 2013). www.meathfieldnames.com

Stiofán Ó Cadhla, *Civilizing Ireland – Ordnance Survey, 1824–1842: Ethnography, Cartography, Translation* (Dublin: Irish Academic Press, 2007).

Patrick J. O'Connor, *Atlas of Irish Place-Names* (County Limerick, Newcastle West: Oireacht na Mumhan, 2001).

Seoirse Ó Dochartaigh, *Inis Eoghain – The Island of Eoghan: The Place-Names of Inishowen* (Privately published, 2010, new edition 2014).

William O'Kane, *Heather, Peat and Stone: The Parishes and Townlands of Tyrone* (Dungannon: Irish World, 1992).

Mícheál Ó Mainnín, *Annexing Irish Names to the English Tongue: Language Contact and the Anglicisation of Irish Place-Names*, Paul Walsh Memorial Lecture, vol. 2 (Maynooth, School of Celtic Studies, NUI, 2017).

Des O'Reilly, *An Illustrated Guide to the Placenames of Ulster* (Belfast: Des O'Reilly and Associates, 2015).

Pádraig Ó Riain, Diarmuid Ó Murchadha and Kevin Murray, *Historical Dictionary of Gaelic Placenames/Foclóir Stairiúil Áitainmneacha na Gaeilge*, 7 vols to date (London: Irish Texts Society, 2003–08).

Robert Sharpe and Charles McAllister, *A Glimpse of Glenarriffe* (Privately published, 1997).

William J. Smyth, *Map-making, Landscapes and Memory: A Geography of Colonial and Early Modern Ireland, c. 1530–1750* (Cork: Cork University Press, 2006).

Michael Swift, *Historical Maps of Ireland* (London: Chartwell Books, 1999).

Donna Thornton and Kevin Murray, *Bibliography of Publications on Irish Placenames* (London/Dublin: Irish Texts Society, 2011).

Una Walsh and Kevin Murphy (eds), *Kick Any Stone: Townlands, People and Stories of Forkhill Parish* (Forkhill: Mullaghbawn Community Association, 2003).

Essays, articles and review articles

Angélique Day, 'Ordnance Survey Memoirs 1830–40', *Donegal Annual*, 35 (1983).

—, 'Portraying Donegal: The Ordnance Survey Memoirs' *Donegal Annual*, 51 (1999).

Dónall Mac Giolla Easpaig, 'The place-names of Rathlin Island', *Ainm: A Journal of Name Studies*, iv (1989–90), pp 3–89.

—, 'Placenames and Early Settlement in County Donegal' in William Nolan, Liam Ronayne and Mairead Dunleavy (eds), *Donegal: History and Society* (Dublin: Geography Publications, 1995), pp 149–82.

—, 'Placenames of County Galway' in Gerard Moran and Raymond Gillespie (eds), *Galway: History and Society* (Dublin: Geography Publications, 1996), pp 795–815.

Conor McDowell, 'Ordnance Survey Memoirs' in *Familia: Ulster Genealogical Review*, no. 24 (2008).

Tom McErlean, 'The Irish townland system of landscape organisation', in Reeves-Smyth, Terence; Hamond, Fred (eds), *Landscape Archaeology in Ireland* (Oxford: BAR British Series, 116, 1983), pp 315–39.

Deirdre Flanagan, 'Settlement terms in Irish place-names,' *Onoma*, xvii (1972–3), pp 157–69, plus 5 maps.

—, 'Ecclesiastical elements in place-names', *Bull. Ulster Place-Name Soc.* (2nd series) iv (1981–2), pp 69–75.

Patrick McKay, 'Scots influences on Ulster townland names', *Ainm: A Journal of Name Studies*, ix (2009), pp 1–26.

—, 'Scots elements in Ulster minor place-names', *Ainm: A Journal of Name Studies*, xiii (2016), pp 1–18.

—, 'Some Belfast Place-Names', *Nomina*, xxiii (2000), pp 49–54.

—, 'Belfast Place-Names and the Irish Language' in Fionntán de Brún (ed.), *Belfast and the Irish Language* (Dublin: Four Courts Press, 2006), pp 15–35.

John J. Marshall, 'Origin of Some of Belfast's Street-Names'. Compiled from articles by Marshall and others published in the *Belfast Telegraph* and other papers from *c.* 1940–57.

Brian Mitchell, 'The Ordnance Survey Memoirs: A Source for Emigration in the 1830s' *History Ireland*, Vol. 4, No. 4 (Winter 1996).

Kay Muhr, 'Territories, People and Place-names in Co. Armagh', in A. J. Hughes and William Nolan (eds), *Armagh: History and Society* (Dublin: Geography Publications, 2001), pp 295–331.

—, 'The Early Place-names of County Armagh', *Seanchas Ard Mhacha*, xix, part 1 (2002), pp 1–54.

—, 'The Mountain of Slewtrim or Bessy Bell', *Journal of the West Tyrone Historical Society*, vol. i, 1 (2007), pp 72–9.

—, 'Review article on Michael Swift's *Historical Maps of Ireland*' in *Ainm: A Journal of Name Studies*, x (2009), pp 138–45.

—, 'Place-names and Scottish clan traditions in north-east County Antrim', in J. D. McClure, J. M. Kirk and M. C. Storrie (eds), *A Land that Lies Westward: Language and Culture in Islay and Argyll*, (Edinburgh: Birlinn, 2009), pp 79–102.

—, 'Queen Medb in place-names', in Gregory Toner and Séamus Mac Mathúna (eds), *Ulidia 3: Proceedings of the third international conference on the Ulster Cycle of tales, University of Ulster, Coleraine, 22–25 June, 2009 – In memoriam Patrick Leo Henry* (Berlin: Curach Bhán, 2013), pp 49–73.

—, 'Deer Park Farms, Parish of Tickmacrevan: Towards the older place-name landscape of Glenarm and area', in C. J. Lynn and J. A. McDowell *et al, Deer Park Farms: the Excavation of a Raised Rath in the Glenarm Valley, Co. Antrim* (Belfast: NIEA, 2011), pp 62–76.

—, 'English place-names in Ireland', in J. Carroll, and D. N. Parsons (eds), *Perceptions of Place: Twenty-First-Century Interpretations of English Place-Name Studies* (Nottingham: EPNS, 2013), pp 355–97.

—, 'The Place-names of County Fermanagh', in Claire Foley and Ronan McHugh, *An Archaeological Survey of County Fermanagh*, 2 vols (Belfast: NIEA, 2014), pp 17–54.

Paul Tempan, 'Surveys of Irish Place-names: a Bibliography', *Ainm: A Journal of Name Studies*, x (2009), pp 157–234.

Gregory Toner, 'Settlement and settlement terms in medieval Ireland: ráth and lios', *Ainm: A Journal of Name Studies*, viii (1998–2000), pp 1–40.

—, 'Baile: settlement and landholding in medieval Ireland', *Éigse: A Journal of Irish Studies*, xxxiv (2004), pp 25–43.

Mary Wack, 'Ordnance Survey Memoirs: Filling out family stories' *Familia: Ulster Genealogical Review*, no. 25 (2009).

Useful websites

www.logainm.ie/ (administrative names)
www.meitheal.logainm.ie (minor names)
www.placenamesni.org (administrative and minor names)
https://thecore.com/seanruad/ (1851 townland list)
https://www.townlands.ie/
https://geohive.ie/
www.ulsterplacename.org

Ulster Place-Name Society – Street Names Project
UPNS: https://www.ulsterplacename.org/street-names-project

Ulster Place-Name Society – Hidden Heritage of Holy Wells
www.ulsterplacename.org/holy-wells/2020/7/1/introducing-holy-wells

The Primary (Griffith's) Valuation of Tenements (*c.* 1848–64)
http://www.askaboutireland.ie/griffith-valuation/
www.failteromhat.com/griffiths.php

Tithe Applotment Books
http://titheapplotmentbooks.nationalarchives.ie/search/tab/home.jsp
www.nidirect.gov.uk/services/search-pronis-ecatalogue (accessed via PRONI's eCatalogue)

Ordnance Survey Ireland
https://www.osi.ie/

Ordnance Survey of Northern Ireland
www.nidirect.gov.uk/campaigns/ordnance-survey-of-northern-ireland

The Northern Ireland Sites and Monuments Record (NISMR)
www.communities-ni.gov.uk/services/sites-and-monuments-record

National Townland and Historical Map Viewer (Ordnance Survey Ireland)
https://geohive.maps.arcgis.com/apps/webappviewer/index.html?id=9def898f708b47f19a8d8b7088a100c4

Ordnance Survey Maps Online (Northern Ireland)
www.nidirect.gov.uk/services/search-proni-historical-maps-viewer
www.communities-ni.gov.uk/services/historic-environment-map-viewer

Maps of the escheated counties of Ireland, 1609
http://digital-library.qub.ac.uk/digital/collection/p15979coll8/id/168/rec/3
https://blogs.qub.ac.uk/specialcollections/newly-digitised-maps-of-the-escheated-counties-of-ireland-1609

An update of E. I. Hogan's *Onomasticon Goedelicum* (1910)
http://research.ucc.ie/doi/locus

Gasaitéar na hÉireann/Gazetteer of Ireland
www.logainm.ie/Eolas/Data/Brainse/gasaitear-na-heireann.pdf

The Northern Ireland Place-Name Project

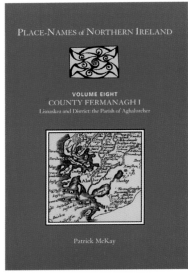

The Northern Ireland Place-Name Project, based in the Department of Irish and Celtic Studies at Queen's University Belfast, has been researching the origins and meanings of local place-names since 1987. Early spellings of the names discussed are abstracted from historical sources, and these provide the evidence necessary to reconstruct the original form of the name and trace its development down to modern times. Names are dealt with in the traditional civil parish units so that both historical and local context may become clear.

In particular, the value of these volumes to local and family historians is the fact that a very significant proportion of Irish place-names have a personal name element. Thus, they can be a quite unique and ingenious way of trying to identify a family's link to a particular locality, especially when there is a lack of other documentary evidence to aid the searcher.

The project website **www.placenamesni.org** presents a searchable database which contains over 30,000 place-names in total (i.e. townland names, settlements and names of physical features, etc). The database contains a gazetteer of these names which was compiled by project researchers from maps and other sources. The gazetteer continues to grow; additions are constantly required as new names are coined in urban landscapes and as traditional names (which have previously been unrecorded) are discovered in the field.

These names originated in a variety of languages: primarily Irish historically (e.g Belfast < Beal Feirste), but with increasing numbers of names in English (Draperstown) and Scots (Glarryford) appearing on record since the Plantation of Ulster in the seventeenth century. There are also names which originated in Old Norse (Strangford) or which indicate contact with, or knowledge of, other languages such as French (Pomeroy). The corpus of historical citations for these names currently stands at approximately 130,000 references in the database; these citations have been abstracted from a wide variety of sources stretching over the best part of two millennia.

The database is searchable by map (which facilitates the location of a name in its geographical context) and by place-name or place-name element (which provides the historical profile of the name and further discussion of it, where available). It is also possible to search for an historical form and to establish to what modern name it has been assigned in the database.

The current research phase (2017–2020) involves providing a suggested origin for every townland name (of whatever linguistic origin) in Northern Ireland, and the preliminary townland analyses are published on the project website, www.placenamesni.org. It builds on the significant amount of work on townlands in previous phases of the project, some of which is published in *The Place-Names of Northern Ireland* series (1992–2004). The volumes still in print are distributed by Ulster Historical Foundation.

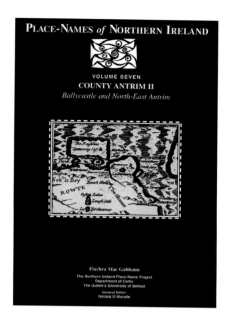

ANTRIM

County Antrim I (series vol. 4)
by Patrick McKay
The Baronies of Toome, covering: Barony of Toome Upper – parishes of Cranfield, Drummaul, Duneane, Grange of Ballyscullion, Grange of Shilvodan; Barony of Toome Lower – parishes of Ahoghill, Craigs, Kirkinriola, Portglenone

County Antrim II (series vol. 7)
by Fiachra Mac Gabhann
Ballycastle and North-East Antrim, covering: Barony of Cary – parishes of Armoy, Ballintoy, Culfeightrin, Grange of Drumtullagh, Ramoan, Rathlin Island

DERRY/LONDONDERRY

County Derry I (series vol. 5)
by Gregory Toner
The Moyola Valley, covering: Barony of Loughinsholin – parishes of Ballynascreen, Ballyscullion, Desertmartin, Kilcronaghan, Killelagh, Maghera, Termoneeny

DOWN

County Down I (series vol. 1)
by Gregory Toner and Mícheál B. Ó Mainnín
Newry and South-West Down, covering: the parish of Newry; Barony of Upper Iveagh – parishes of Clonallan, Donaghmore, Drumgath, Kilbroney, Warrenpoint

County Down II (series vol. 2)
by J. Hughes and R. J. Hannan
The Ards, covering: Barony of Upper Ards – parishes of Ardkeen, Ardquin, Ballyphilip, Ballytrustan, Ballywalter, Castleboy, Inishargy, St. Andrew's and Ballyhalbert, Slanes, Witter; Barony of Lower Ards – parishes of Bangor, Donaghadee, Grey Abbey, Newtownards

County Down III (series vol. 3)
by Mícheál B. Ó Mainnín
The Mournes, covering: Barony of Mourne – parish of Kilkeel; Barony of Upper Iveagh (Lower Half) – parishes of Clonduff, Kilcoo

County Down IV (series vol. 6)
by Kay Muhr
North-West Down/Iveagh, covering: Barony of Iveagh – parishes of Aghaderg, Annaclone, Donaghcloney, Dromore, Drumballyroney, Garvaghy, Magheralin, Magherally, Moira, Seapatrick, Tullylish

FERMANAGH

County Fermanagh I (series vol. 8)
by Patrick McKay
Lisnaskea and District: the Parish of Aghalurcher, covering: Barony of Magherastephana – parishes of Aghalurcher (Fermanagh portion), Aghalurcher (Tyrone portion)

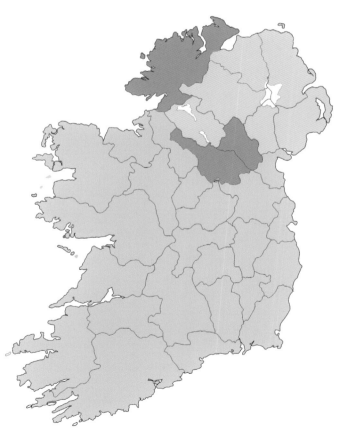

Map of the island of Ireland with the province of Ulster highlighted. The area shaded in light purple is modern Northern Ireland; the three counties coloured purple are Cavan, Donegal and Monaghan

Ordnance Survey Memoirs of Ireland

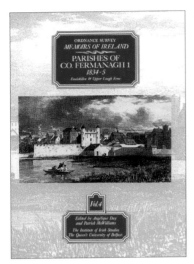

The Ordnance Survey Memoirs of Ireland provide a uniquely detailed history of the northern half of Ireland immediately before the Great Famine. The Memoirs were mainly written in the 1830s, to accompany the 6-inch Ordnance Survey Maps, yet, except for the parish of Templemore, Co. Londonderry, they were not actually published at the time. In the 1990s the Institute of Irish Studies at Queen's University Belfast published the memoirs in forty volumes covering the northern counties of Ireland.

The Memoirs act as a nineteenth-century Domesday Book, and are essential to the understanding of the cultural heritage of our communities. They document the landscape and situation, buildings and antiquities, land holdings and population, employment and livelihood of the parishes. Importantly, for many parishes in counties Antrim and Londonderry they provide the names of emigrants during this period, the year they left and the port to which they emigrated. Learn not just about the houses of your ancestors, but the type of work they did, the schools they were educated in, the churches where they worshipped, the roads they got about on, and more.

All 40 volumes remain in print and are distributed by Ulster Historical Foundation.

Ordnance Survey Memoirs by county

ANTRIM

Co. Antrim I (series vol. 2)
Ballymartin, Ballyrobert, Ballywalter, Carnmoney, Mallusk

Co. Antrim II (series vol. 7)
Blaris (Lisburn), Derryaghy, Drumbeg, Lambeg

Co. Antrim III (series vol. 10)
Carncastle, Killyglen, Island Magee, Kilwaughter, Larne

Co. Antrim IV (series vol. 13)
Ardclinis, Dunaghy, Dundermot, Inispollan, Layd, Loughguile, Newtown Crommelin, Racavan, Skerry, Tickmacrevan

Co. Antrim V (series vol. 16)
Ballymoney, Ballyrashane, Ballywillin, Billy, Derrykeighan, Drumtullagh, Dunluce, Kilraghts

Co. Antrim VI (series vol. 19)
Ballyscullion, Connor, Cranfield, Drummaul, Duneane, Shilvodan

Co. Antrim VII (series vol. 21)
Aghagallon, Aghalee, Ballinderry, Camlin, Glenavy, Lough Neagh, Magheragall, Magheramesk, Tullyrusk

Co. Antrim VIII (series vol. 23)
Ahoghill, Ballyclug, Finvoy, Killagan, Kirkinriola, Rasharkin

Co. Antrim IX (series vol. 24)
Armoy, Ballintoy, Culfeightrin, Ramoan, Rathlin Island

Co. Antrim X (series vol. 26)
Glynn, Inver, Kilroot, Templecorran

Co. Antrim XI (series vol. 29)
Antrim, Doagh, Donegore, Kilbride

Co. Antrim XII (series vol. 32)
Ballycor, Ballylinny, Ballynure, Glenwhirry, Raloo, Rashee

Co. Antrim XIII (series vol. 35)
Carmavy, Killead, Muckamore, Nilteen, Templepatrick, Umgall

Co. Antrim XIV (series vol. 37)
Carrickfergus

ARMAGH

Co. Armagh (series vol. 1)
Ballymore, Ballymyre, Clonfeacle, Creggan, Drumcree, Eglish, Forkill, Jonesborough, Keady, Kilclooney, Killevy, Killyman, Kilmore, Loughgall, Loughgilly, Montiaghs, Mullaghbrack, Newtownhamilton, Seagoe, Shankill, Tartaraghan, Tynan

DERRY/LONDONDERRY

Co. Londonderry I (series vol. 6)
Arboe (part), Artrea, Ballinderry, Ballyscullion, Magherafelt, Termoneeny

Co. Londonderry II (series vol. 9)
Balteagh, Drumachose (Newtownlimavady)

Co. Londonderry III (series vol. 11)
Aghanloo, Magilligan (Tamlaghtard), Dunboe

Co. Londonderry IV (series vol. 15)
Dungiven

Co. Londonderry V (series vol. 18)
Maghera, Tamlaght O'Crilly

Co. Londonderry VI (series vol. 22)
Aghadowey, Agivey, Ballyrashane, Kildollagh,
Macosquin

Co. Londonderry VII (series vol. 25)
Bovevagh, Tamlaght Finlagan

Co. Londonderry VIII (series vol. 27)
Desertoghill, Errigal, Killelagh, Kilrea

Co. Londonderry IX (series vol. 28)
Cumber (Upper & Lower)

Co. Londonderry X (series vol. 30)
Banagher

Co. Londonderry XI (series vol. 31)
Ballynascreen, Desertlyn, Desertmartin,
Kilcronaghan, Lissan

Co. Londonderry XII (series vol. 33)
Ballyaghran, Ballywillin, Coleraine, Killowen

Co. Londonderry XIII (series vol. 34)
Clondermot

Co. Londonderry XIV (series vol. 36)
Faughanvale

DONEGAL

Co. Donegal I (series vol. 38)
Clondavaddog, Clonmany, Culdaff, Desertegney,
Donagh, Killygarvan, Kilmacrenan, Lough Swilly
(with Burt and Inch), Mevagh, Mintiaghs (Bar of
Inch), Moville, Muff, Tullyaughnish

Co. Donegal II (series vol. 39)
Clonleigh, Convoy, Conwal, Donaghmore, Donegal,
Drumhome, Glencolumbkille, Inishkeel, Kilbarron,
Killea and Taughboyne, Killymard, Kilteevoge, Leck,
Raphoe, Raymoghy, Taughboyne, Templecarn,
Tullaghhobegley, Urney

DOWN

Co. Down I (series vol. 3)
Clonallan, Clonduff, Donaghmore, Drumballyroney,
Drumgath, Drumgooland, Kilbroney, Kilcoo, Kilkeel,
Kilmegan, Newry, Warrenpoint

Co. Down II (series vol. 7)
Ardkeen, Ardquin, Ballyhalbert (St Andrew's),
Ballyphilip, Ballytrustan, Ballywalter, Bangor,
Castleboy, Comber, Donaghadee, Drumbeg,
Drumbo, Dundonald, Grey Abbey,
Holywood, Inishargy, Killinchy,
Kilmood, Knockbreda, Newtownards,
Saintfield, Slanes, Tullynakill, Witter

Co. Down III (series vol. 12)
Aghaderg, Annaclone, Annahilt, Blaris (Lisburn)
Donaghcloney, Dromara, Dromore, Garvaghy,
Hillsborough, Magheralin, Magherally, Moira,
Seapatrick, Shankill, Tullylish

Co. Down IV (series vol. 17)
Ardglass, Ballee, Ballyculter, Ballykinler, Bright,
Down, Dunsfort, Inch, Kilclief, Killyleagh, Kilmore,
Loughinisland, Magheradrool, Rathmullan, Saul

FERMANAGH

Co. Fermanagh I (series vol. 4)
Aghalurcher (part), Aghavea, Clones,
Derrybrusk, Drummully, Enniskillen,
Galloon, Kinawley, Tomregan (part)

Co. Fermanagh II (series vol. 14)
Belleek, Boho, Cleenish, Derryvullan,
Devenish, Drumkeeran, Inishmacsaint,
Killesher, Magheracross, Magheraculmoney,
Rossorry, Templecarn, Trory

TYRONE

Co. Tyrone I (series vol. 5)
Aghalurcher (part), Ardstraw, Cappagh,
Clogher, Donacavey, Donaghedy, Dromore,
Drumragh, Kilskeery, Leckpatrick, Longfield
(West, East & Lower), Skirts of Urney &
Termonamongan

Co. Tyrone II (series vol. 20)
Aghaloo, Artrea, Ballinderry, Ballyclog, Bodoney,
Carnteel, Clogherny, Clonoe, Desertcreat, Donaghenry,
Drumglass, Errigal Keerogue, Kildress, Killeeshill,
Killyman, Lissan, Pomeroy, Tamlaght, Tullyniskan

SOUTH ULSTER (series vol. 40)

Co. Cavan: Drumgoon, Drumlumman, Drung,
Enniskeen, Killdrumsherdan, Laragh

Co. Leitrim: Manorhamilton Union

Co. Louth: Ballymascanlan, Carlingford, Castletown

Co. Monaghan: Aghabog, Aghnamullen, Ballybay,
Clontibret, Currin, Donagh, Donaghmoyne,
Ematris, Errigal Trough, Inishkeen, Killanny, Kilmore,
Magheracloone, Magheross, Monaghan, Muckno,
Tydavnet, Tyholland (Tehallan)

Co. Sligo: Emlaghfad, Killoran, Kilvarnet, Kilmacteigue

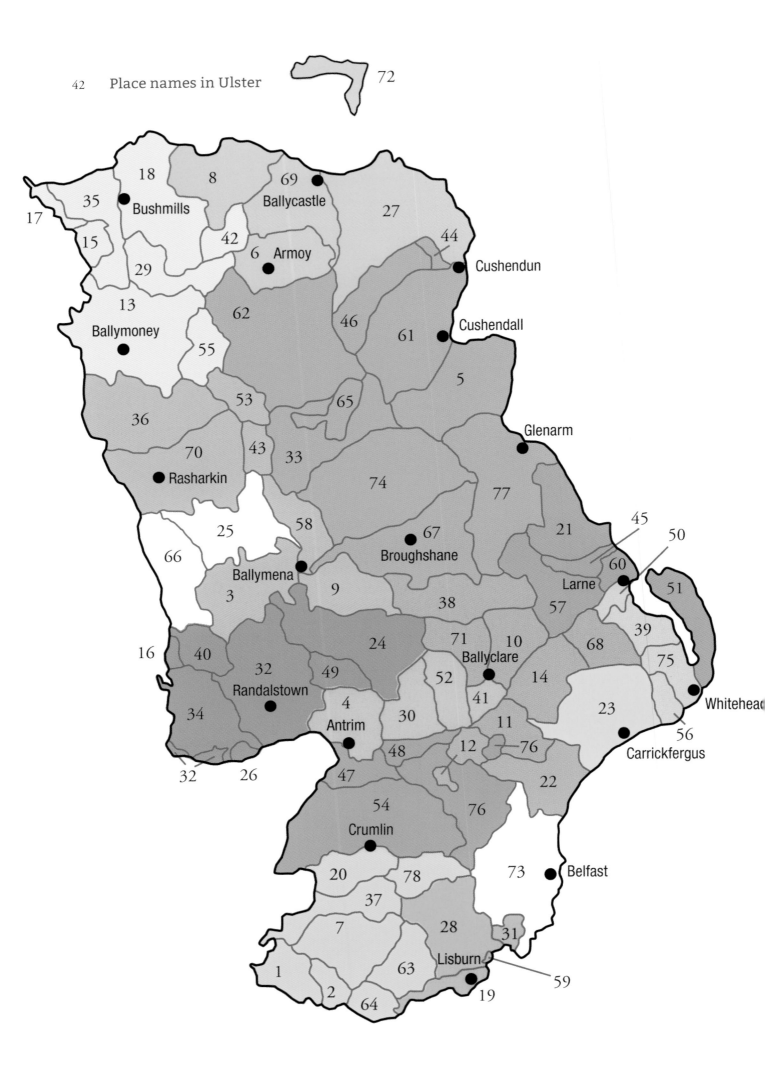

72

18   8   69
35   Bushmills   Ballycastle
17   27
15   42   44
29   6 Armoy   Cushendun
13   62   46   Cushendall
Ballymoney   61
55   5
53   65
36   Glenarm
70   43   33   77
Rasharkin   74   21   45
25   58   67   50
66   Broughshane   60
Ballymena   9   38   57   Larne   51
3   39
16   40   24   71   10   75
32   49   52   Ballyclare   14   68
Randalstown   41   23   Whitehead
34   4   30   11   56
32   26   Antrim   48   12   76   Carrickfergus
47   22
54   76
Crumlin
20   78   73   Belfast
37
7   28   31
1   63   Lisburn
2   64   19   59

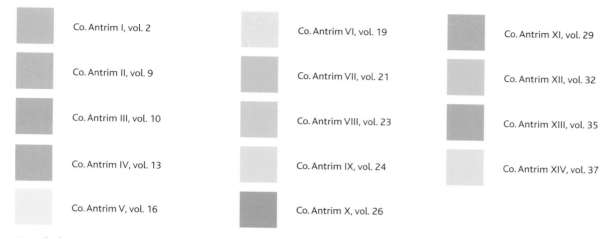

Co. Antrim I, vol. 2	Co. Antrim VI, vol. 19	Co. Antrim XI, vol. 29
Co. Antrim II, vol. 9	Co. Antrim VII, vol. 21	Co. Antrim XII, vol. 32
Co. Antrim III, vol. 10	Co. Antrim VIII, vol. 23	Co. Antrim XIII, vol. 35
Co. Antrim IV, vol. 13	Co. Antrim IX, vol. 24	Co. Antrim XIV, vol. 37
Co. Antrim V, vol. 16	Co. Antrim X, vol. 26	

Craigs (25) and Portglenone (66) were originally part of Ahoghill (3).

Road sign near Mallusk, County Antrim

CIVIL PARISHES IN COUNTY ANTRIM

1 Aghagallon
2 Aghalee
3 Ahoghill
4 Antrim
5 Ardclinis
6 Armoy
7 Ballinderry
8 Ballintoy
9 Ballyclug
10 Ballycor
11 Ballylinny
12 Ballymartin
13 Ballymoney
14 Ballynure
15 Ballyrashane
16 Ballyscullion
17 Ballywillin
18 Billy
19 Blaris
20 Camlin

21 Carncastle
22 Carnmoney
23 Carrickfergus
24 Connor
25 Craigs
26 Cranfield
27 Culfeightrin
28 Derryaghy
29 Derrykeighan
30 Donegore
31 Drumbeg
32 Drummaul
33 Dunaghy
34 Duneane
35 Dunluce
36 Finvoy
37 Glenavy
38 Glenwhirry
39 Glynn
40 Grange of Ballyscullion

41 Grange of Doagh
42 Grange of Drumtullagh
43 Grange of Dundermot
44 Grange of Inispollan
45 Grange of Killyglen
46 Grange of Layd
47 Grange of Muckamore
48 Grange of Nilteen
49 Grange of Shilvodan
50 Inver
51 Island Magee
52 Kilbride
53 Killagan
54 Killead
55 Kilraghts
56 Kilroot
57 Kilwaughter
58 Kirkinriola
59 Lambeg
60 Larne

61 Layd
62 Loughguile
63 Magheragall
64 Magheramesk
65 Newtown Crommelin
66 Portglenone
67 Racavan
68 Raloo
69 Ramoan
70 Rasharkin
71 Rashee
72 Rathlin
73 Shankill
74 Skerry
75 Templecorran
76 Templepatrick
77 Tickmacrevan
78 Tullyrusk

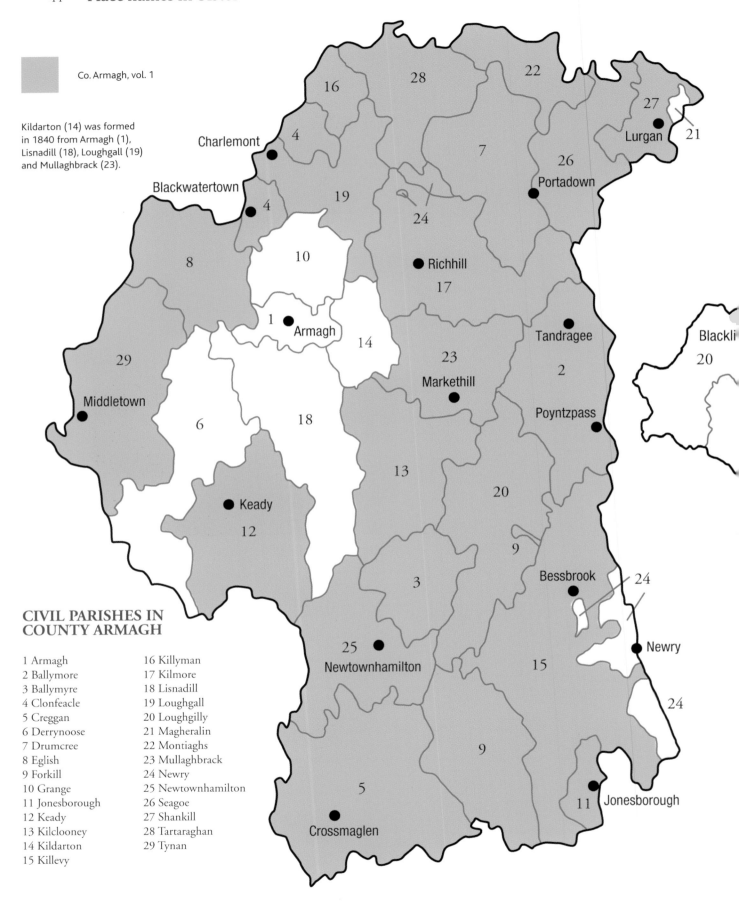

Co. Armagh, vol. 1

Kildarton (14) was formed
in 1840 from Armagh (1),
Lisnadill (18), Loughgall (19)
and Mullaghbrack (23).

Charlemont

Blackwatertown

Lurgan

Portadown

Richhill

Tandragee

Markethill

Poyntzpass

Blackli

Middleton

Keady

Bessbrook

Newry

Newtownhamilton

Jonesborough

Crossmaglen

**CIVIL PARISHES IN
COUNTY ARMAGH**

1 Armagh
2 Ballymore
3 Ballymyre
4 Clonfeacle
5 Creggan
6 Derrynoose
7 Drumcree
8 Eglish
9 Forkill
10 Grange
11 Jonesborough
12 Keady
13 Kilclooney
14 Kildarton
15 Killevy

16 Killyman
17 Kilmore
18 Lisnadill
19 Loughgall
20 Loughgilly
21 Magheralin
22 Montiaghs
23 Mullaghbrack
24 Newry
25 Newtownhamilton
26 Seagoe
27 Shankill
28 Tartaraghan
29 Tynan

CIVIL PARISHES IN COUNTY CAVAN

1 Annagelliff
2 Annagh
3 Ballintemple
4 Bailieborough
5 Ballymachugh
6 Castlerahan
7 Castleterra
8 Crosserlough
9 Denn
10 Drumgoon
11 Drumlane
12 Drumlumman
13 Drumreilly
14 Drung
15 Enniskeen
16 Kilbride
17 Kildallan
18 Kildrumsherdan

19 Killashandra
20 Killinagh
21 Killinkere
22 Kilmore
23 Kinawley
24 Knockbride
25 Larah
26 Lavey
27 Loughan or Castlekeeran
28 Lurgan
29 Moybolgue
30 Mullagh
31 Munterconnaught
32 Scrabby
33 Shercock
34 Templeport
35 Tomregan

South Ulster, vol. 40

Excerpt from map of Ireland by John Senex, 1720
LIBRARY OF THE OIREACHTAS, DUBLIN

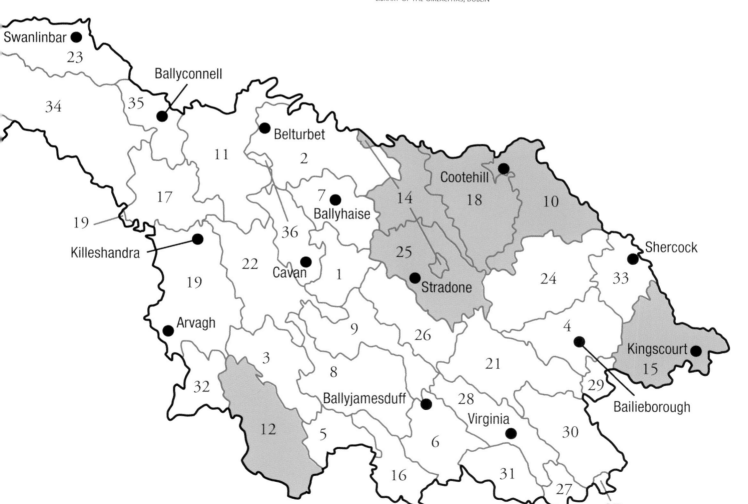

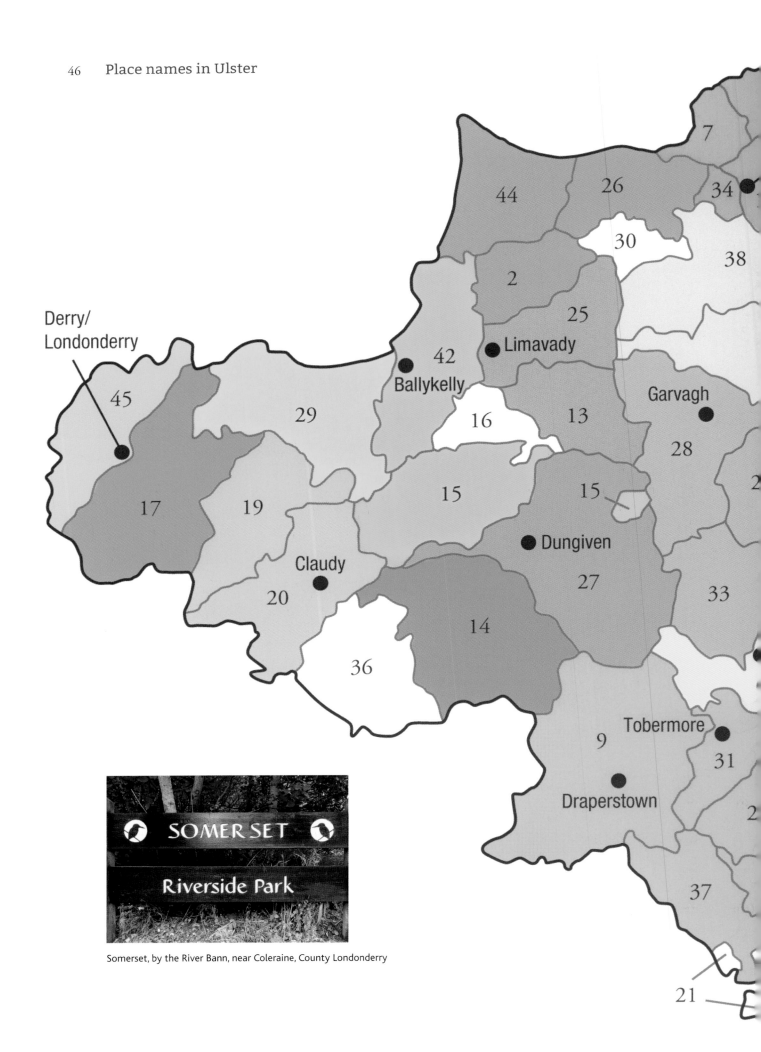

Somerset, by the River Bann, near Coleraine, County Londonderry

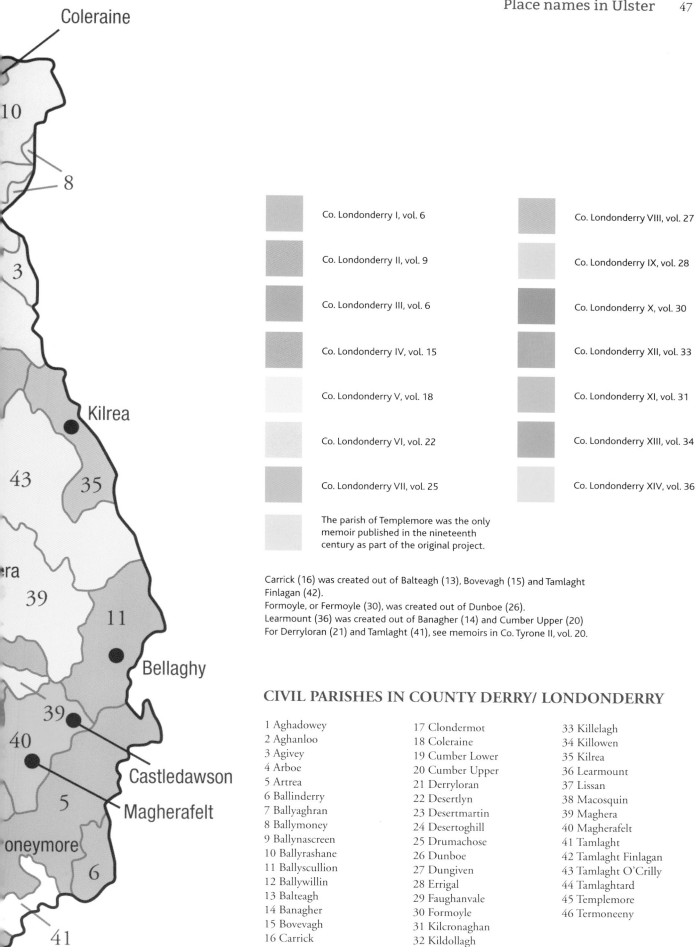

Co. Londonderry I, vol. 6

Co. Londonderry II, vol. 9

Co. Londonderry III, vol. 6

Co. Londonderry IV, vol. 15

Co. Londonderry V, vol. 18

Co. Londonderry VI, vol. 22

Co. Londonderry VII, vol. 25

Co. Londonderry VIII, vol. 27

Co. Londonderry IX, vol. 28

Co. Londonderry X, vol. 30

Co. Londonderry XII, vol. 33

Co. Londonderry XI, vol. 31

Co. Londonderry XIII, vol. 34

Co. Londonderry XIV, vol. 36

The parish of Templemore was the only memoir published in the nineteenth century as part of the original project.

Carrick (16) was created out of Balteagh (13), Bovevagh (15) and Tamlaght Finlagan (42).
Formoyle, or Fermoyle (30), was created out of Dunboe (26).
Learmount (36) was created out of Banagher (14) and Cumber Upper (20)
For Derryloran (21) and Tamlaght (41), see memoirs in Co. Tyrone II, vol. 20.

CIVIL PARISHES IN COUNTY DERRY/ LONDONDERRY

1 Aghadowey
2 Aghanloo
3 Agivey
4 Arboe
5 Artrea
6 Ballinderry
7 Ballyaghran
8 Ballymoney
9 Ballynascreen
10 Ballyrashane
11 Ballyscullion
12 Ballywillin
13 Balteagh
14 Banagher
15 Bovevagh
16 Carrick

17 Clondermot
18 Coleraine
19 Cumber Lower
20 Cumber Upper
21 Derryloran
22 Desertlyn
23 Desertmartin
24 Desertoghill
25 Drumachose
26 Dunboe
27 Dungiven
28 Errigal
29 Faughanvale
30 Formoyle
31 Kilcronaghan
32 Kildollagh

33 Killelagh
34 Killowen
35 Kilrea
36 Learmount
37 Lissan
38 Macosquin
39 Maghera
40 Magherafelt
41 Tamlaght
42 Tamlaght Finlagan
43 Tamlaght O'Crilly
44 Tamlaghtard
45 Templemore
46 Termoneeny

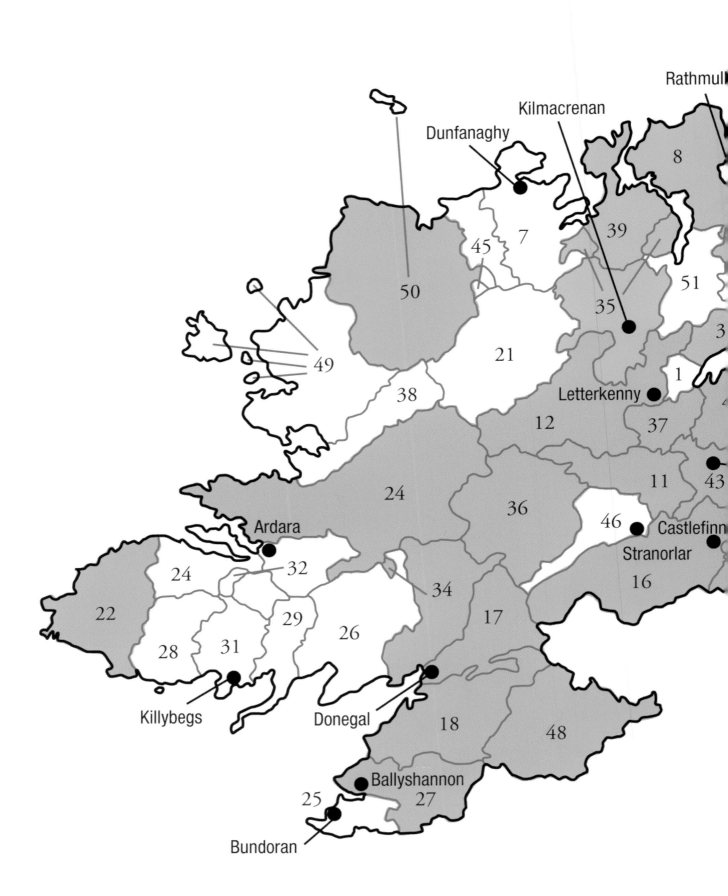

Rathmull

Kilmacrenan

Dunfanaghy

8

39

45   7

50

35

51

3

21

Letterkenny

1

49

38

12

37

24

36

11   43

Ardara

46   Castlefinn

32

Stranorlar

34

16

22

29

17

24

28   31   26

48

18

Killybegs

Donegal

Ballyshannon

25   27

Bundoran

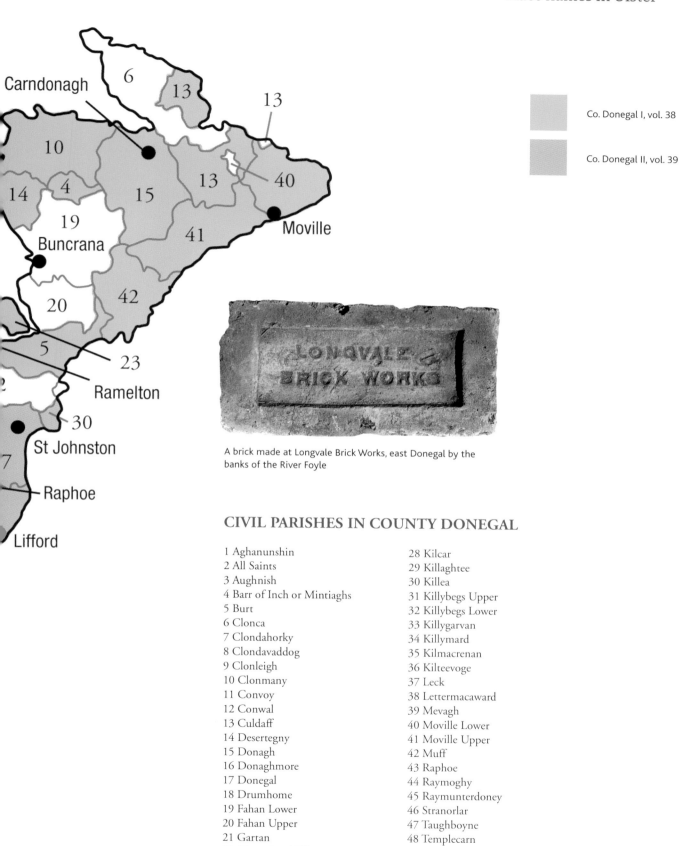

Co. Donegal I, vol. 38

Co. Donegal II, vol. 39

A brick made at Longvale Brick Works, east Donegal by the banks of the River Foyle

CIVIL PARISHES IN COUNTY DONEGAL

1 Aghanunshin
2 All Saints
3 Aughnish
4 Barr of Inch or Mintiaghs
5 Burt
6 Clonca
7 Clondahorky
8 Clondavaddog
9 Clonleigh
10 Clonmany
11 Convoy
12 Conwal
13 Culdaff
14 Desertegny
15 Donagh
16 Donaghmore
17 Donegal
18 Drumhome
19 Fahan Lower
20 Fahan Upper
21 Gartan
22 Glencolumbkille
23 Inch
24 Inishkeel
25 Inishmacsaint
26 Inver
27 Kilbarron

28 Kilcar
29 Killaghtee
30 Killea
31 Killybegs Upper
32 Killybegs Lower
33 Killygarvan
34 Killymard
35 Kilmacrenan
36 Kilteevoge
37 Leck
38 Lettermacaward
39 Mevagh
40 Moville Lower
41 Moville Upper
42 Muff
43 Raphoe
44 Raymoghy
45 Raymunterdoney
46 Stranorlar
47 Taughboyne
48 Templecarn
49 Templecrone
50 Tullaghobegley
51 Tullyfern

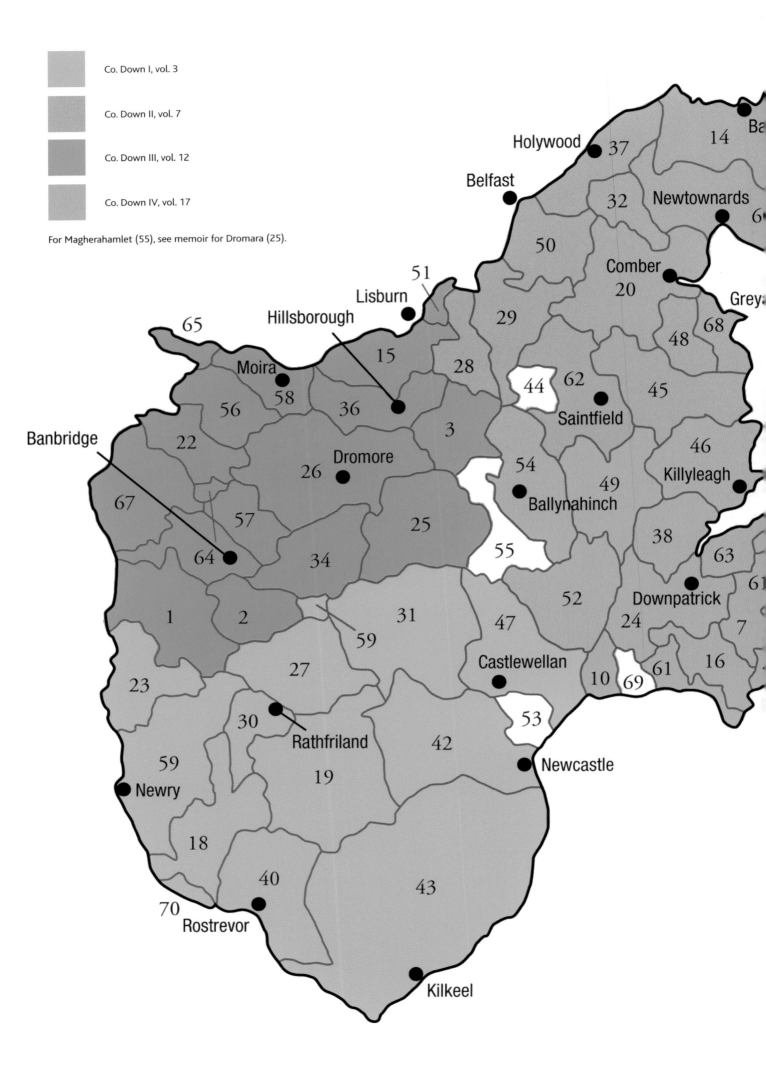

Co. Down I, vol. 3

Co. Down II, vol. 7

Co. Down III, vol. 12

Co. Down IV, vol. 17

For Magherahamlet (55), see memoir for Dromara (25).

Holywood 37 14 Ba

Belfast 32 Newtownards 6

50 Comber 20 Grey

51 29 48 68

Lisburn 44 62 45

Hillsborough 15 28 Saintfield

65 Moira 36 3 46

58 54 Killyleagh

56 Dromore 49

Banbridge 22 26 55 38 63

67 57 25 52 Downpatrick 61

64 34 31 47 24 7

1 2 59 10 69 16

23 27 Castlewellan 53

30 42

59 Rathfriland 19 Newcastle

Newry

18

40 43

70 Rostrevor

Kilkeel

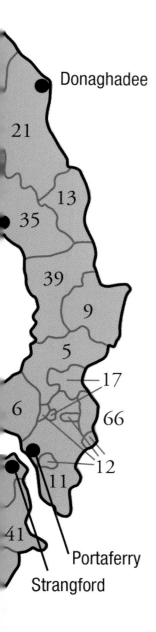

'A Survey of the Town of Downpatrick in the County of Down
... by James Maguire, 1708'

PRONI, D477/1

CIVIL PARISHES IN COUNTY DOWN

1 Aghaderg	19 Clonduff	37 Holywood	55 Magherahamlet
2 Annaclone	20 Comber	38 Inch	56 Magheralin
3 Annahilt	21 Donaghadee	39 Inishargy	57 Magherally
4 Ardglass	22 Donaghcloney	40 Kilbroney	58 Moira
5 Ardkeen	23 Donaghmore	41 Kilclief	59 Newry
6 Ardquin	24 Down	42 Kilcoo	60 Newtownards
7 Ballee	25 Dromara	43 Kilkeel	61 Rathmullan
8 Ballyculter	26 Dromore	44 Killaney	62 Saintfield
9 Ballyhalbert	27 Drumballyroney	45 Killinchy	63 Saul
10 Ballykinler	28 Drumbeg	46 Killyleagh	64 Seapatrick
11 Ballyphilip	29 Drumbo	47 Kilmegan	65 Shankill
12 Ballytrustan	30 Drumgath	48 Kilmood	66 Slanes
13 Ballywalter	31 Drumgooland	49 Kilmore	67 Tullylish
14 Bangor	32 Dundonald	50 Knockbreda	68 Tullynakill
15 Blaris	33 Dunsfort	51 Lambeg	69 Tyrella
16 Bright	34 Garvaghy	52 Loughinisland	70 Warrenpoint
17 Castleboy	35 Grey Abbey	53 Maghera	
18 Clonallan	36 Hillsborough	54 Magheradrool	

CIVIL PARISHES IN COUNTY FERMANAGH

1 Aghalurcher
2 Aghavea
3 Belleek
4 Boho
5 Clones
6 Cleenish
7 Derrybrusk
8 Derryvullan
9 Devenish
10 Drumkeeran
11 Drummully
12 Enniskillen

13 Galloon
14 Inishmacsaint
15 Killesher
16 Kinawley
17 Magheracross
18 Magheraculmoney
19 Rossorry
20 Templecarn
21 Tomregan
22 Trory

Headstone, Aghalurcher graveyard, County Fermanagh

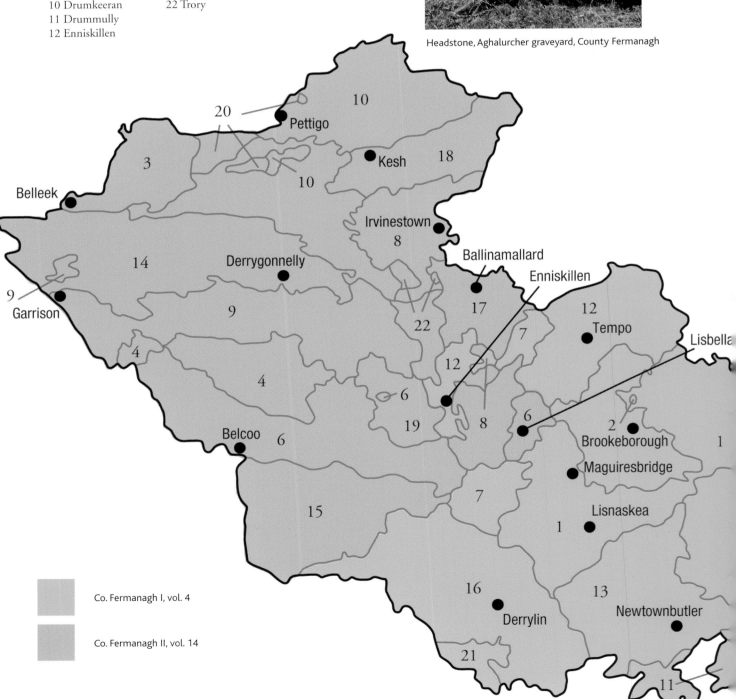

Co. Fermanagh I, vol. 4

Co. Fermanagh II, vol. 14

South Ulster, vol. 40

CIVIL PARISHES IN COUNTY MONAGHAN

1 Aghabog
2 Aghnamullen
3 Ballybay
4 Clones
5 Clontibret
6 Currin
7 Donagh
8 Donaghmoyne
9 Drummully
10 Drumsnat
11 Ematris
12 Errigal Trough
13 Inishkeen
14 Killanny
15 Killeevan
16 Kilmore
17 Magheracloone
18 Magheross
19 Monaghan
20 Muckno
21 Tedavnet
22 Tehallan
23 Tullycorbet

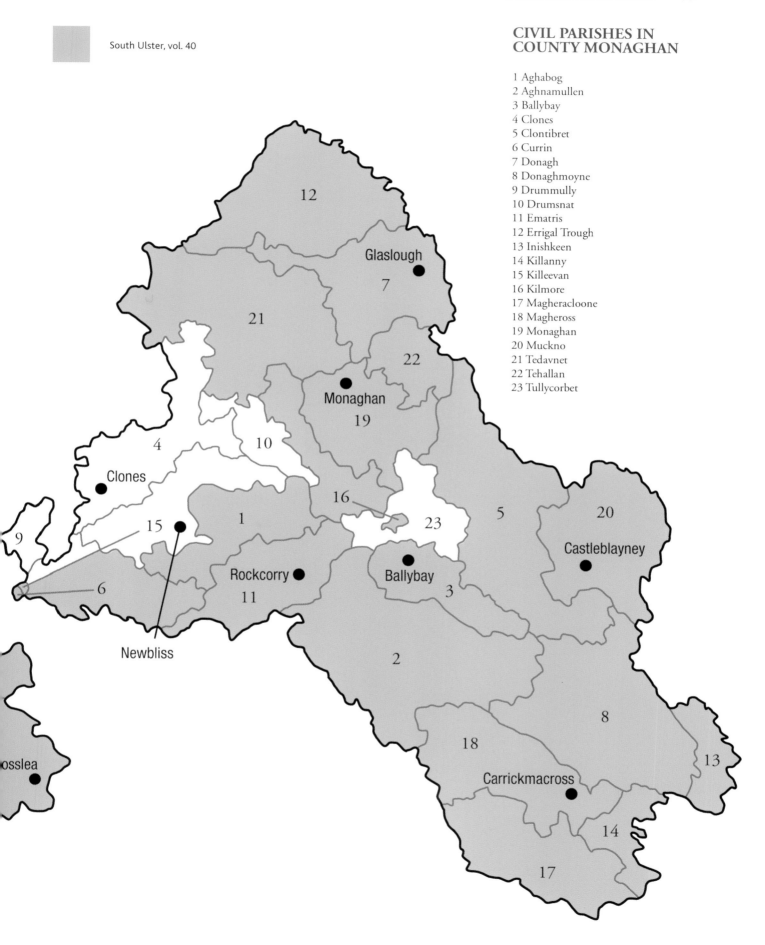

12

Glaslough

7

21

22

Monaghan

19

4

10

Clones

16

1

15

9

5

20

Castleblayney

6

Rockcorry

11

Ballybay

23

3

Newbliss

2

8

18

13

osslea

Carrickmacross

14

17

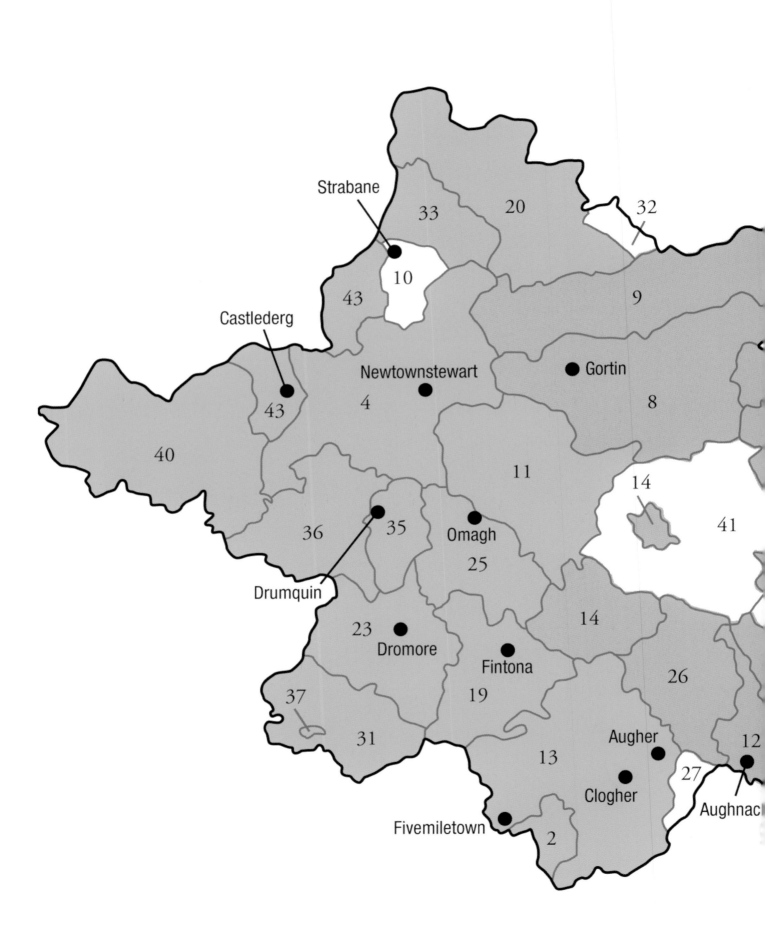

Townland marker, Bready, County Tyrone

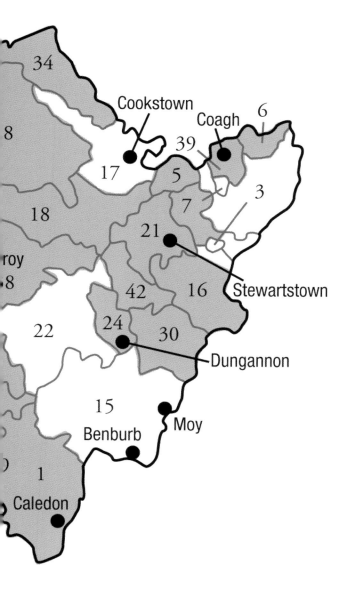

Co. Tyrone I, vol. 5

Co. Tyrone II, vol. 20

CIVIL PARISHES IN COUNTY TYRONE

1 Aghaloo
2 Aghalurcher
3 Arboe
4 Ardstraw
5 Artrea
6 Ballinderry
7 Ballyclog
8 Bodoney Lower
9 Bodoney Upper
10 Camus-juxta-Mourne
11 Cappagh
12 Carnteel
13 Clogher
14 Clogherny
15 Clonfeacle
16 Clonoe
17 Derryloran
18 Desertcreat
19 Donacavey
20 Donaghedy
21 Donaghenry
22 Donaghmore

23 Dromore
24 Drumglass
25 Drumragh
26 Errigal Keerogue
27 Errigal Trough
28 Kildress
29 Killeeshil
30 Killyman
31 Kilskeery
32 Learmount
33 Leckpatrick
34 Lissan
35 Longfield East
36 Longfield West
37 Magheracross
38 Pomeroy
39 Tamlaght
40 Termonamongan
41 Termonmaguirk
42 Tullyniskan
43 Urney

The publication of this work was made possible by the generosity of the following individuals. Ulster Historical Foundation would like to thank all patrons, donors and subscribers for their support.

Patrons

Mark Adair
Roisin Adams
Margaret Bannon
Norbert Bannon
Carol Tweedale Bardon
Dr Justin Basquille
S. J. Connolly
John Waddell and Jane Conroy
Ronald Denham
Barbara Fagan
Colin D. Gowdy
Bronagh Hinds
Diane Hughes-Hart
John Hunter

Oliver and Rosie Johnston
Michael and Edna Longley
David McCormick
Rosemary McCreery
Vivian McIver
Niall McSperrin
Máire Neary
Dónall and Máire Ó Baoill
Mary Schranz
Dr Patrick Speight
Brian M. Walker
John Waugh
Paul Weir
Colin Wilson

Donors

Daniel Bardon
Jane Bardon
David Bass
Brenda Collins
Gerald Dawe
Angélique Day
Thomas Deas
Roger and Valerie Dixon
The Very Revd. Gregory Dunstan
Terry Eakin
Trevor Edwards
Winifred Glover
John Hagan
David and Deirdre Hayton
Frances Heales
Seamus Higgins
Diane Kelly
Dr Alec Lyons
James Marshall
John McKimmon
Dr Richard McMinn

Gerry Mullan
Eddis Nicholl
Anne Odling-Smee, CBE
David O'Dwyer
Trevor and Sheila Parkhill
James Patterson
Nuala Quinn
Patrick Fintan Quinn
Andrew Remedios
W. N. B. Richardson
William J. Roulston
Peter Smyth
Linda Stephens
Anne Tannahill
Patricia Thimell
Rosana Trainor
Anna Tweedale
Charlotte Tweedale
Patrick Tweedale
Ruth Tweedale
Anonymous

Subscribers

Bruce Adaire
Genevieve Ahearne
Robert Anselmi
Eoin Bairéad
Dorothy Barry
D. I. Bartlett
Gerry and Ann Begley
Kathleen Bhattacharyya
Hilary Bell
Sandra Bennett
Galen A. Black
June Blackburn
Maurice Blease
Thomas F. Boyce
Terence Bradley
Michael Brady
Patricia Brown
Rodney Brown
Sharon Brown
Fran van Bruggen
Deirdre Byrne
Gerard Byrne
Eric Cahill
Christie Calhoun
Dr G. Johnston Calvert
John Cantley
Barbara Carnaghan
Harold Clark
Brigid Clements
Yvonne Cowieson
David C. Cranston
Gerard Crawford
Megan Crook
Ian Crossan
Tony Crowe
Michael Crozier
Jennifer Cunningham
David Currie
Joanna Nic Bhrain Curry
Brian Dane
Chris Dart
Lois Dean
Jill Deane
Stanislaus Dempsey
Anne Devlin and Chris Parr
Peter Devlin
Desmond Doherty
David S. Dunlop
Mr Robert Epperson
Michael Esler
Steve Ewing

Robert Ewing
Arthur Fife
Gerard Finnegan
Joan Fox
Hazel Francey
Eamonn Furey
Christian Gering
Alastair Gillies
Peter Gilmore
James Hall
Brett Hannam
Brooke Harlowe
Paul Harris
Carol and Richard Hawkins
Elizabeth Hayes
William Hayes
Carol Hemmersmeier
Janice L. Henry
Peter Hill
Trevor Hodgett
Brendan Holland
Charles Howell
Chris Hudson and Isabella Evangelisti
Charmaine Huey
William Hurford
Ann Igoe
Rorke and Ingrid Bryan
David and Maureen Irwin
Ernest Jackson
Oliver Johnston
Rosie Johnston
Alan Jones
Donna Jones
Arnita Jones
Andrew Kane
Andrew Kelly
Daniel Kennedy
Norman Kerr
Millie Knox
Mary Jane Kuffner Hirt
Cynthia J. Lear
Rosalind LeComte
Tony Lenihan
Professor Sheena Lewis
Helen Livingstone
Gordon Lucy
William Lutton
Dr Alec Lyons
Virginia MacLatchy
Richard Maclean
Robert J. Macoubrie
Ian Magowan

C. F. Martin
Howard Mathieson
Marion Maxwell
Mary Maxwell-Irving
Ross McAllen
Gwen McCamley
Timothy McCorriston
Denis McCoy
Ken McCracken
Pamela McCrory
Kelly McCullar
Susan McCullough
Babs and Tom McDaid
James McElherne Sr.
Melvin McFadden
Ruth McFarland
Kathleen McGale
Anne McGrath
Medbh and John McGuckian
Edward McInairnie
Marg McIntyre
Julie McKane
Willie McKee
Rodney McKelroy
Stephanie McKenna
Mary Jane McKitterick
James McKnight
Karen McKnight
Sandra McLaughlin
Wilfrid McLean
David McMenemy
Jean McNulty
A. J. McReynolds
Douglas McTavish
Graeme McVerry
Patricia McWilliam
Hugh Miller
Tom Moore
Barbara Morris
John Mulvenna
Elgin Murphy
Joseph Murray
Nonie and Frank Murray
Colm Murray-Cavanagh
Gareth Neighbour
Marilyn Nevala
Ernest Nixon
Feargal Ó Béarra
Mary O'Brien
Peter O'Brien
Angela O'Donnell
John O'Gorman
Jack O'Hare
Marcas Ó Murchú

Philip O'Rawe
Geraldene O'Reilly
Russell Ó Ríagáin
Gail Orr
W. George Orr
James Orr
Gary Pallister
Charles Palmer
Marcus Patton
Sue Piper
Annabel Price
Michael Fintan Quinn
Dr Aoife Quinn
Conor Quinn
Eoghan Quinn
Niamh Quinn
George Rea
Christine Reaburn
Andrea (Reilly) Reeve
Austin Reid
Don Revels
Mark Richardson
Sharon Rivers and Trevor Moore
Jane Rogers
Susan Rogers
John Patrick Rooney
Elizabeth Russell
Paul Ryan
Daniel Sandoval
Christine Sanger
Richard Sayre
Brendan Scott
Helen Shimek
James Smith
Lolly Spence
J. Steele
Joseph Steele
Madeleine Stewart
William Stewart
Colin Strain
Peter and Barbara Tame
Jack Tenison
J. I. Thompson
John Thompson
James Turner
Ulster Historical Foundation
Mary Margaret Van Damme
Anthony Vesey
Jennifer Vormwald
Richard Wilson
Susan Wilson
Sharen Wixom
Daniel Yarrow

A few small comments

The spelling of all languages changes over time, and medieval spellings of similar date for the Early Kingdoms of Ulster p. 7 would be:

Used in text	Recommended spelling
Tír Amhlaimh	Clann Amhlaoibh
Leth Cathail	Leath Cathail
Dál Riata	Dál Riada
Dartraige	Dartraighe
Latharne	Lathairne
Dál nAraide	Dál nAraidhe

As well as spelling, translation is a tricky business. Some word definitions:

ceapach (p. 15)   'plot of land cleared for tillage', from *ceap* 'stump'.

duach (p. 11)   *dumhach* 'mound'('sand dune' began as a special usage).

mug (p. 7)   'slave', current spelling is *mogh*.

riabhach (p. 8)   'streaked, striped, brindled, grizzled, speckled' – think of granite.

tor (p. 15)   'tower' in the sense of a rock pinnacle, not a settlement word.

More recent thinking on some of the names (*see **www.placenamesni.org** for further discussion):

Antrim*   Ir. *Aontreibh*, 'single house/habitation', referring to an early monastery. The name was later reinterpreted as *Aontroim*, 'single ridge'.

Bangor*   Ir. *Beannchar*, perhaps meaning 'place of points'.

Divis   Ir. *Dubhais*, 'black ridge'.

Doagh   Ir. *Dumhach*, 'mound'.

Donegore   Ir. *Dun Ó gCorra*, 'fort of the Corrs or descendants of *Corra*'.

Letterbreen   Ir. *Leitir Bruíne*, perhaps 'hillside of the dwelling/fairy fort'.

Lisburn*   'origin uncertain'. No need for a query at 'fort of the gamblers'.

Gweebarra*   Ir. *Gaoth Beara*, 'estuary of the *Bior*'. An old word for river, see McKay, 2007.

Killough   Ir. *Cill Locha*, 'church of the lough', the sea inlet now called Killough Harbour.

Malone*   Ir. *Maigh Luain* '*Luan*'s plain'.

Rathkenny   Ir. *Ráth Cainnigh*, '*Cainneach*'s fort'.

Strabane   Ir. *An Srath Bán*, 'the white river-holm'.

Townlands

The fascinating subject of townlands in Ireland can be explored further through the publications and websites listed in Further reading (see pp 35–7).

A useful starting point into the subject can be founded in the Land Units (Territorial Divisions in Ireland) Appendix in the *Place-Names of Northern Ireland* volumes (see p. 39); and the Land Units section of the Northern Ireland Place-Name website: www.placenamesni.org/landunits.php

A help sheet can also be downloaded from the Public Record Office of Northern Ireland's website under the Local History series information leaflets: 'Local History – 1 The Townland' www.nidirect.gov.uk/publications/local-history-series-information-leaflet-1-townland